Concise Guide to
Information Literacy

Obviously, a man's judgment cannot be better than the information on which he has based it.

—Arthur Hays Sulzberger, publisher of the
New York Times from 1935 to 1961

Concise Guide to Information Literacy

Scott Lanning

LIBRARIES UNLIMITED

AN IMPRINT OF ABC-CLIO, LLC
Santa Barbara, California • Denver, Colorado • Oxford, England

Library of Congress Cataloging-in-Publication Data

Lanning, Scott.
  Concise guide to information literacy / Scott Lanning.
       p. cm.
  Includes bibliographical references and index.
  ISBN 978-1-59884-949-3 (pbk.) — ISBN (invalid) 978-1-61069-191-8 (ebook)
  1. Information literacy.   I. Title.
  ZA3075.L36   2012
  020—dc23   2011049229

ISBN: 978-1-59884-949-3
EISBN: 978-1-61069-191-8

16 15 14   2 3 4 5

This book is also available on the World Wide Web as an eBook.
Visit www.abc-clio.com for details.

Libraries Unlimited
An Imprint of ABC-CLIO, LLC

ABC-CLIO, LLC
130 Cremona Drive, P.O. Box 1911
Santa Barbara, California 93116-1911

This book is printed on acid-free paper ∞

Manufactured in the United States of America

To my wife for her invaluable support and encouragement.

Contents

List of Figures xi

CHAPTER 1: Information and Information Literacy 1
    What Is Information? 1
    What Is Information Literacy? 2
    Why Is Information Literacy Important? 3
    Vocabulary. 6
    Questions. 6
    Assignment 6

CHAPTER 2: The Information Need and Types of Information. 7
    The Information Need. 7
        Refining the Research Question. 8
    Knowing Where to Look. 9
    Categories of Information 10
        Primary versus Secondary Information Sources 10
        Scholarly versus Popular Information Sources 11
        Current versus Historical Information Sources 12
    Formats of Information Sources 12
        Print 13
        Electronic 13
    Types of Information Sources. 13
        Reference/Background Sources 14
        Books 14
        News Sources 15
        Magazines. 16
        Journals. 16
        Indexes 17

Vocabulary. 18
Questions. 18
Assignment 18

CHAPTER 3: Finding Information 21
What Is a Database? 21
    Free Databases 22
    Fee Databases. 23
Searching Databases 23
    Basic Search. 24
    Advanced Search 24
Language of the Search. 25
    Keyword Searching and Synonyms 25
    Subject Searching and Field Searching 26
Mechanics of the Search 27
    Boolean Operators 27
    Proximity and Phrase Searching. 30
    Nesting 31
    Truncation and Wildcards. 32
    Using Help Screens 34
    Refining the Search 34
Vocabulary. 36
Questions. 36
Assignment 36

CHAPTER 4: Utilizing the Library Catalog and Resources .39
Searching the Library Catalog 39
Retrieving Materials 40
Utilizing Print Sources 42
Utilizing Electronic Sources .43
Vocabulary. 43
Questions. 44
Assignment 44

CHAPTER 5: Utilizing Library Databases. 45
Choosing a Database. 45
    Citation, Abstract, and Full-Text Databases. 46
Utilizing Electronic Sources .47
Vocabulary. 48
Questions. 48
Assignment 49

CHAPTER 6: Utilizing the Web. 51
Web Search Engines 51

Basic Searching. 51
Advanced Searching 52
Metasearch Engines 53
Utilizing Web Sources. 54
Vocabulary. 54
Questions. 54
Assignment 55

CHAPTER 7: Librarians and Library Services. 57
The Librarian. 57
Research Help 58
Library Instruction 58
Interlibrary Loan 58
Vocabulary. 59
Questions. 59
Assignment 59

CHAPTER 8: Evaluation and the Research Process. .61
What Is Evaluation? 61
Evaluating Your Research Process 62
Search Statement 62
Keywords 63
Database Selection 63
Research Question 64
Vocabulary. 65
Questions. 65
Assignment 65

CHAPTER 9: Evaluating Information 67
Relevance 67
Purpose 67
Scope and Depth. 68
Style 68
Validity 70
Timeliness. 70
Accuracy. 70
Authority 72
Vocabulary. 74
Questions. 74
Assignment 74

CHAPTER 10: Evaluating Your Product 77
Organization 77
Logic 78

Proofreading 78

Vocabulary. 79

Questions. 79

Assignment 79

CHAPTER 11: Using Information. 81

Communicating Information. 81

Using Information 82

Intellectual Property, Copyright, and Fair Use. .82

Plagiarism. 84

Quoting, Paraphrasing, and Summarizing Information 84

Citing Your Information 85

Learning from the Experience. 87

Vocabulary. 88

Questions. 88

Assignment 88

Works Cited 91

Index 95

List of Figures

FIGURE 1.1. Topic Worksheet. 6

FIGURE 2.1. Information Creation and Access. 10

FIGURE 2.2. Time to Publication. 15

FIGURE 2.3. Topic and Aspects Worksheet. 19

FIGURE 3.1. Record from a Database. 22

FIGURE 3.2. Basic Search Screen. 24

FIGURE 3.3. Advanced Search Screen. 24

FIGURE 3.4. Keyword Worksheet. 25

FIGURE 3.5. Synonym Worksheet. 26

FIGURE 3.6. And Operator. 28

FIGURE 3.7. Earthquakes and Tsunamis and Models. 29

FIGURE 3.8. Or Operator. 29

FIGURE 3.9. Not Operator. 30

FIGURE 3.10. Search Worksheet with Search Strategy. 34

FIGURE 3.11. Search Worksheet with Broadened Search Strategy. 34

FIGURE 3.12. Search Worksheet with Narrowed Search Strategy. 35

FIGURE 3.13. Search Statement Worksheet. 37

FIGURE 4.1. Dewey Decimal and Library of Congress
Call Number for *The Planets*. 42

FIGURE 4.2. Library Catalog Worksheet. 44

FIGURE 5.1. Database Search Worksheet. 49

FIGURE 6.1. Internet Search Worksheet. 55

FIGURE 9.1. Information Evaluation Worksheet. 75

FIGURE 10.1. Paper Evaluation Worksheet. 80

FIGURE 11.1. Book Citation in Two Formats. 86

FIGURE 11.2. Journal Citation in Two Formats. 86

FIGURE 11.3. Citation Worksheet. 88

CHAPTER 1

Information and Information Literacy

What Is Information?

This book is about information literacy. What it is, why it is important, and how you can become information literate. So what is information literacy? We will start by taking a look at information. Information is defined as: "Data which has been recorded, classified, organized, related, or interpreted within a framework so that meaning emerges" (Information 2003).

Is the following information?

- 16895

No. By our definition, it is data. We have no context in which to understand this number. It could refer to many things. If you saw this number on the windshield of a car in the lot of an auto dealership, is it still data? No, not any more. Now it is information. We know that the number is the price of that car. It has a framework that gives it meaning. The car is a specific make, model, and year with a certain set of options and dealer profit that determine the price. If it is a used car, then that price also reflects mileage and condition.

Information comes from many sources. We are surrounded by it. Television, the Internet, and billboards are all sources of information. Your friend telling you what happened at a party the other night is giving you information. That information may be given to you in person, over the phone, via Twitter, or on Facebook.

Information is more than just reporting what has happened. Information can also be discovered and created. A researcher who develops a new metal alloy or a scientist who finds a medicinal property of a plant has created information. It is also created by you when you write a paper and support your arguments with the research of others.

We all have some understanding of what it means to be *literate*. It means we can read and write. Literate also means "having knowledge or skill in a specified field" (Literate 2011). So being information literate means having knowledge about information. We can check the price of that car on a site like Edmunds (http://www.edmunds.com) and determine whether it is a good deal or overpriced. This is an example of information literacy.

What Is Information Literacy?

Information literacy is the ability to find, evaluate, and use information efficiently, effectively, and ethically to answer an information need. An information need can be anything from determining a fair price for a good used car to developing a new product. Writing a research paper is an information literacy process. It involves finding and applying information to answer your research questions to either support or disprove your hypothesis. To do this well, you want to evaluate the information you use to ensure its quality while recording the publication information you need to give credit to the people whose ideas you use.

The Association of College and Research Libraries (ACRL) has their own criteria of what information literacy is all about, and they are collected in a document called *Information Literacy Competency Standards for Higher Education*. It lists the skills you should have and what you should be able to do when you learn about information literacy:

- *Determine the extent of information needed.* If you need only a quick fact or definition, then you do not have to consult multiple sources and find 10 research articles. You only need to consult an encyclopedia or dictionary. If you have to write a paper, then using an encyclopedia will not give you enough information to answer your research question.

- *Access the needed information effectively and efficiently.* You know where to look and how to look for the information you need, and you can find it quickly.

- *Evaluate information and its sources critically, and incorporate selected information into one's knowledge base.* You can determine if the information you found is appropriate to your research and whether the information, or its source, is good or bad, and you learn from all that information you gathered.

- *Use information effectively to accomplish a specific purpose.* You write your research paper, develop your new process or market a product, and accomplish your task well.

- *Understand the economic, legal, and social issues surrounding the use of information, and access and use information ethically and legally* (Association of College and Research Libraries 2000). You understand the concept of intellectual property and know the consequences of plagiarizing someone else's ideas. You know how to cite your sources.

> —Excerpted from *Information Literacy Competency Standards for Higher Education* by the Association of College and Research Libraries, a division of the American Library Association, copyright © 2000 American Library Association. Available for download at http://www.acrl. org/ala/mgrps/divs/acrl/standards/informationliteracy competency.cfm. Used with permission.

In this book, we focus on these ideas to help you become information literate. Right now, however, we need to answer the big question.

Why Is Information Literacy Important?

Librarians have a vested interest in the importance of information literacy. We believe it is a vital skill, and because it relates to our jobs, that is not a surprise. However, there are other people who also believe information literacy is important. For example, colleges and universities are accredited. They are given a stamp of approval from an accrediting agency. These agencies have long lists of standards that the colleges have to meet before they are accredited. This process is designed to ensure that you are or will be getting a quality education.

The Middle States Association of Colleges and Schools, a college accrediting agency, says that a college's course of study should be "designed so that students acquire and demonstrate college-level proficiency in general education, scientific and quantitative reasoning, critical analysis and reasoning, technological competency, and information literacy" (Accreditation 2011). The New England Association of Schools and Colleges states that your college should ensure "that students use information resources and information technology as an integral part of their education" because when you graduate you should be able to demonstrate competency in "the ability for scientific and quantitative reasoning, for critical analysis and logical thinking; and the capability for continuing learning, including the skills of information literacy" (Accreditation 2011).

Accrediting agencies are not the only ones concerned with information literacy. *The Prague Declaration* came from a United Nations Educational, Scientific, and Cultural Organization (UNESCO) supported conference with the National Forum on Information Literacy (http://infolit.org), a not-for-profit organization with an international membership dedicated to promoting information literacy, and the National Commission on Libraries and Information Science, which is a U.S. government agency now called the Institute of Museum and Library Services (http://www.imls.gov). The conference had representatives from 23 countries who agreed on the following:

- The creation of an *information society* is key to social, cultural, and economic development of nations and communities, institutions, and individuals in the 21st century and beyond.

- *Information literacy* encompasses knowledge of one's information concerns and needs and the ability to identify, locate, evaluate, organize, and effectively create, use, and communicate information to address issues or problems at hand; it is a prerequisite for participating effectively in the information society and is part of the basic human right of lifelong learning.

- Information literacy, in conjunction with access to essential information and effective use of information and communication technologies, plays a leading role in reducing the inequities within and among countries and peoples and in promoting tolerance and mutual understanding through information use in multicultural and multilingual contexts.

- Governments should develop strong interdisciplinary programs to promote information literacy nationwide as a necessary step in closing the digital divide through the creation of an information literate citizenry, an effective civil society, and a competitive workforce (UNESCO 2003).

We end this section with a list from a group of librarians. This list nicely and succinctly summarizes what others have said about why information literacy is important. The American Association of School Librarians (AASL) developed *Standards for the 21st-Century Learner*, which is their list of things you should be able to do by the time you graduate from high school.

Learners Use Skills, Resources, and Tools To Do the Following:

- Inquire, think critically, and gain knowledge.

- Draw conclusions, make informed decisions, apply knowledge to new situations, and create new knowledge.

- Share knowledge and participate ethically and productively as members of our democratic society.

- Pursue personal and aesthetic growth (American Association of School Librarians 2007).

> —Excerpted from *Standards for the 21st-Century Learner* by the American Association of School Librarians, a division of the American Library Association, copyright © 2007 American Library Association. Available for download at www.ala.org/aasl/standards. Used with permission.

These are the outcomes of information literacy. This is what you should be able to do. Information literacy is important for your education. It will enable you to be a better student and get better grades. It is important to your career as you will be a better employee and help your company be more competitive and productive.

It is important to your life as you will be able to make better decisions informed by facts that will help you with everything from purchases to personal finances. It will help you become a lifelong learner as you will be able to learn new skills and adapt to changes in your workplace and society. It will make you a better global citizen as you will be able to participate in an informed and engaged manner in our democratic society, and you will have a greater understanding of the world at large.

If these reasons still are not enough to explain why information literacy is important, then consider the following two quotes. Richard Dawkins, a prominent evolutionary biologist said, "What lies at the heart of every living thing is not a fire, not warm breath, not a 'spark of life'. It is information, words, instructions" (1986, 112). James Gleick, a Pulitzer Prize nominated author stated in his book *The Information: A History, a Theory, a Flood,* "Information is what our world runs on: the blood and the fuel, the vital principle" (2011, 8). We are creatures of information, built by information, powered by information and consuming information. Shouldn't we know what information is and how to sift through the billions of bits of information to find the pieces we need?

Vocabulary

creation of information

data

information

information literacy

information need

lifelong learning

sources of information

Questions

Where does information come from?

Who creates information?

What does it mean to participate in our democratic society?

What is a "global citizen"?

Why is lifelong learning important?

Assignment

Pick three broad topics that can be expressed in a few words. See the example in Figure 1.1. Later you will pick one of these three topics and explore specific concepts within it.

TOPIC IDEAS
1. Climate change
2. Illegal drugs
3. Eating disorders

Figure 1.1: Topic Worksheet.

CHAPTER 2

The Information Need and Types of Information

In this chapter and the following chapters, we use the ACRL *Competency Standards* (Association of College and Research Libraries 2000) as our outline of material to be covered. We start with determining the extent of the information needed and how to access the information effectively and efficiently.

The Information Need

As stated earlier, this is the question that needs an answer. In the context of school, this is the research question that you need to answer in your paper or project. It is the hypothesis that you will seek to prove or disprove, or the thesis you will explore. In your personal life, it could be finding the best cell phone deal for your intended use or the cheapest price on the best HD TV. For your professional life, it could be finding how much money the average consumer spends on premium chocolates, which are the top brands, and whether the market is big enough for another competitor.

The information need may not be big. You may need to know only a fact like the magnitude of the largest earthquake every recorded. You may need a little background like knowing what the Richter scale is and what the difference is between a 4 and a 5 on that scale. Both of these questions can be answered quickly and from one source. You may even find the answer to both questions in the same source. When you read your background source, you will discover that the Richter scale has been replaced with the moment magnitude scale (Richter Magnitude Scale 2011).

But if you need information on the state of the art in the prediction of earthquakes, you may need additional facts and background information, plus the latest research articles so you can understand what an earthquake is, how the magnitude is measured, animals' sensitivity to earthquakes, how science is trying to predict them, and what kind of success they are having. This is no longer a simple information need. It is a complex question that requires a lot of information from different sources, and the answer may not be definitive.

You have your research question: What is the state of the art in the prediction of earthquakes? Recognizing that your question is big, that it cannot be answered by a single source, that it has multiple facets, and that it requires background information in order to understand all aspects of it is a very good beginning.

Refining the Research Question

As you begin to explore your topic, you may want or need to modify your research question or hypothesis based on the amount and type of information you find. If you are finding too much information, you may need to narrow your focus and look at a specific aspect of your original thesis. If there is too little information, then you will need to broaden your topic. There are no hard and fast numbers that describe too much or too little information, but it is safe to say that if you find so many items that you do not know where to begin or so few that you do not have enough to even start, then you may need to reexamine your thesis. In addition, if the information you are finding is of poor quality and unreliable, then you may also need to reexamine your research question. Maybe changing the wording will lead to good quality, reliable sources. Maybe there just is not enough information available on your topic to write a well-reasoned and supported paper. If that is the case, then you simply need to change your question altogether. Your question is not set in stone from the moment you think of it. It is flexible and can change as you explore your topic. We will talk more specifically about narrowing and broadening your search, evaluating your research process, and evaluating the information you found later on in this book. First, we will examine where to look.

Knowing Where to Look

Knowledge is organized into three broad categories: humanities, social science, and science. According to the Merriam-Webster dictionary, the *humanities* are, "the branches of learning . . . that investigate human constructs and concerns as opposed to natural processes . . . and social relations" (Humanities 2011). This definition does triple duty. It mentions the sciences as "natural processes" and the social sciences as "social relations." The humanities include philosophy, language, literature, art, and theater. The social sciences include anthropology, psychology, sociology, and business, while the sciences include chemistry, physics, biology, astronomy, and geology.

Using your previous research question on earthquake prediction, you can see that it falls into the sciences. This will help you determine the information sources you need to use when you begin your research. If you were instead writing a paper about Ancestral Puebloans or Shakespeare, you would want to consult sources in anthropology and literature, respectively.

Knowing the broad discipline of your topic also helps you to know where to look for information. For example, while journals are important in all disciplines, they are especially important to the sciences. The latest discoveries are documented in the journal literature first. In the humanities, the newest idea might be too big to be expressed in a journals article, so it is published in a book. Within the humanities, for example in the arts, the new idea may be expressed as a series of paintings or a dance.

Figure 2.1 illustrates the information process from its creation to its publication. We talked a little about where information comes from in chapter 1. Now we are going to look specifically at a researcher as a creator of information. It starts with ideas. The researcher then develops their ideas by gathering information, running experiments, and informally discussing their ideas with colleagues. They may present those ideas at a conference, then refine and develop them further. At this point, unless we know the person or attended the conference, we do not have access to their ideas or their research. The information that has been generated has only been informally shared. When the researchers *publish* their ideas, that is to say produce a DVD of the recital, post a video of the ballet to YouTube, or have a journal article published, then the information that they created has been shared with the world, and we can gain access to their ideas through those publications and through sources that lead us to them, called *indexes*.

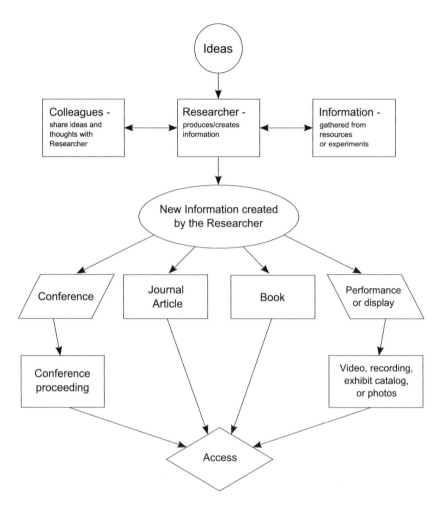

Figure 2.1: Information Creation and Access.

Categories of Information

Information comes in many varieties. We have broken it down into six broad categories of information that can be discussed as pairs that contrast with each other. This makes it easier to understand what each of them entails.

Primary versus Secondary Information Sources

Primary means direct or firsthand (Primary 2011). Primary information, therefore, is firsthand information. It can mean a firsthand account of an event or the results of a research project that is published by the researcher. Secondary information is information that is reported secondhand. For example, when a reporter visits the site of an earthquake and tells you about the event, it is a secondhand report. When that reporter asks a person who experienced the earthquake what it was like, that person's answer is a firsthand or primary account of the event. Diaries and letters are primary sources of information about the person who wrote them. An autobiography is a primary document because it was written by the person in question. A biography is a secondary information source about the person because it was written by somebody else.

A research article is a good example of a primary information source. It is written by the persons who conducted the research project. A secondary information source would be a source that talks about, uses, or summarizes the research done by others. An article about earthquake prediction written by the persons who conducted the research is a primary source. A book that pulls together many primary and secondary sources of information to present an overview of earthquake predictions is presenting information secondhand, making it a secondary source.

Scholarly versus Popular Information Sources

Scholarly information is a research article. It is information that is cited and verified. It is information intended for an academic or specialized audience. It is information that has been peer reviewed and published in a scholarly journal. The peer review process is an important aspect in the publication of a scholarly article. Journals that publish research articles have scholars, or experts in their field, who review the articles that have been submitted for possible publication. This group of scholars or *peers* will read the submissions and decide which ones are good enough to be published in their journal. This peer review process is designed to ensure that only quality articles get published.

It is important to know that while scholarly journals publish scholarly articles that are the results of primary research and primary thinking, not all primary information is scholarly information. An autobiography is primary information, but it is not scholarly. It is popular.

Popular information is information intended for a broad, general audience. It may contain facts that have been verified, and it may have been approved for publication by an editor, but it has not been peer reviewed. For example, an article in *Time magazine* will contain facts that should have been checked. It will be edited and approved for publication, but it is an article that reports on a current event like a demonstration, and it does not require expertise in a field of study to understand. Popular information may have pictures and videos. Scholarly information may have tables and graphs.

Current versus Historical Information Sources

Current and historical are the last two categories of information. Current is easy to understand. It means new, up to date, or the current conditions. Current information varies by discipline. There are exciting astronomical discoveries made all the time. Current information in astronomy needs to have been created very recently to reflect the most up-to-date thinking in the field. In contrast, fields like psychology and sociology move a little slower, and English literature moves even more slowly. An article about human behavior that is 3 years old may have some of the most up-to-date thinking. An article about Shakespeare that is 10 years old may reflect the best modern thought on the bard.

Historical information does not mean old information. It means information about the past, as opposed to the current state of affairs. That information could have been gathered, analyzed, and published yesterday. It is the focus on the history and development of an idea or subject that makes it historical information. You can put together your own historical information by finding information that was current 10, 20, and 50 years ago and comparing it to today to see the changes that have occurred over time. Remember that just because something happened in the past does not mean that there is not current thinking and analysis of it. History, as a field of study, has both current and historical information.

The categories of information can overlap. While it is difficult for something to be both popular and scholarly at the same time, a popular information source could also be primary in nature, while a scholarly source could be secondary and historical. Knowing which categories of information you will need, and how much information you need from each category, will help you with your research. You may want some popular and historical information to help you better understand your topic and to use as the introduction or groundwork for your project, while the bulk of your project will consist of information you gathered from scholarly sources.

Formats of Information Sources

Information comes in different formats. It can be in a physical format or an electronic format. The format of the information is not as important as the quality of the information.

Print

Print is a physical, tangible format for recording information that does not require the use of an electrical device to "read" or extract the information. We read a book, look at a photograph, or flip through a magazine. Information has been coming in print formats ever since man learned how to draw on cave walls. Print sources take up a lot of space. They cost more to publish because of the resources consumed to create the object. They cost more to distribute because of their size and weight. The printing and distribution process all add time to the publication of the information. The advent of electronic formats for information has made print formats less and less popular.

Electronic

Electronic formats include DVDs, MP3s, videocassettes, databases, and the Internet. We need some kind of device to "read" electronic sources. Electronic sources take up very little physical space. One DVD-ROM can hold thousands of books. Tangible versions of electronic sources like DVDs and CDs are subject to the same printing and distribution process as print sources. However, the Internet allows for instantaneous publication and distribution of electronic sources. A publisher may print 1,000 copies of a book and discover that was not enough to meet demand. Then they will have to print additional physical copies of the book. An electronic version of the print book can be accessed by one person or one million people and meet any level of demand without taking up any more space or consuming any more resources. Electronic sources are easily copied and shared with others.

Types of Information Sources

Information is packaged into different types of information sources, and each source influences how much and which categories of information you get. *Scope* is how broad the subject or topics are. An information source with a broad scope covers a very broad topic or lots of topics, and one with a narrow scope may cover only one specific aspect of a topic. *Depth* is how much information on a topic is given in the information source. Sources that lack depth give only a little information, while sources with depth give a lot of information. A dictionary is an example of an information source that has a very broad scope, all the words in a language or field of study, and a very shallow depth, just a brief entry defining a word.

Reference/Background Sources

Background information sources, or reference sources as they are called in a library, are designed to bring you quick facts or provide a short overview of a topic. These sources can be very helpful in your research. They can provide you with a basic understanding of your topic, which will help you focus your question, and provide you with the terminology of your subject, which will help you search and find more information. For these reasons, reference sources are a great place to begin your research. You may not use the information you find in them in your project, and your instructor may not let you, but the start they give you on your research may be invaluable.

Wikipedia and *The New Encyclopædia Britannica* are examples of general reference sources. Their scope is very broad, the whole realm of knowledge. They contain tens of thousands or even millions of articles, but their depth is usually limited. There are reference sources that focus on specific topics like the *McGraw-Hill Encyclopedia of Science and Technology* or the *Routledge Encyclopedia of Philosophy*, or even more specifically, sources such as *Cambridge Illustrated Dictionary of Astronomy* or *The Oxford Handbook of Philosophy of Emotion*. These reference sources have a narrower scope than general encyclopedias, but they have more depth. Still, they do not have as much depth as a book on one of their entries would.

Reference sources are always secondary in nature. They can be popular or scholarly. They usually focus on either current or historical information but may try to do both. There are often many people involved in the writing and editing of reference sources. The very broad scope of reference sources means that they have the greatest length among the different types of information sources. This length and complexity also means that it takes a long time to write and compile the information before it can be published. Reference sources take longer to create in general than any other type of information source. It can take years to produce a reference source. Figure 2.2 illustrates the relative time to publication for each information source.

Books

Books have greater depth and narrower scope than background or reference sources. Their length allows them to cover their topic in great detail. Their scope can be fairly broad, such as the Civil War, or it can be more narrowly focused and cover only General Sherman's battles during the war. Books will give you more information on your topic than any other source of information. It may be too much information,

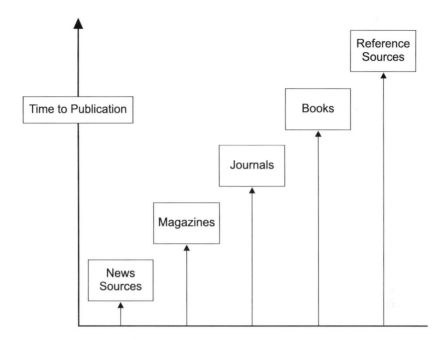

Figure 2.2: Time to Publication.

but you still may need to find specific information within a book for your project.

Books can fall into any category of information. They can be primary or secondary, historical or current, popular or scholarly information sources. Books take the second longest time to reach publication due to their depth and scope.

News Sources

There are many places to get news: the Internet, television, radio, and newspapers. News sources tend to have broad but shallow coverage, similar to background or reference sources. However, they focus on current information, specifically current events, for a broad, popular audience. Articles and reports are usually short and secondary in nature. News sources will help you find current information about the latest discoveries for your topic of research, but it will usually not be enough information, and you may need to find the primary information on which their report was based.

News sources have the shortest time to publication. It can be instantaneous. You can be watching events as they happen on the Internet and on television. Television newscasts report on the events of the day, whereas newspapers report on what happened the day before; both may follow developing stories.

Magazines

Magazines are also geared for a popular audience. They can have a broad scope like *Time*, or they can be narrowly focused like *Rolling Stone* or *Marie Claire*. They usually have more length than a news source, which allows them to cover a topic with more depth. They can feature interviews with important figures within their scope, such as a musician or a fashion designer, and provide primary information. They do not have scholarly articles, so there is no primary research, but secondary reporting. They can have articles on current or historical topics. Their broad coverage and depth may be another good starting point for your research project, and their relatively short time to publication means you can get up-to-date information about events and discoveries. However, their popular nature may preclude their use in a research project.

Journals

Journals publish scholarly articles that have been peer reviewed. Scholarly articles are written by experts and are intended for students and other experts in that field of study. They detail experiments and cite the sources used in the research. Journals have a narrow scope, a specific field or sub-field of study, and they often have great depth because articles can be long and very narrowly focused. You may find a number of journal articles that have a similar thesis to yours. They may serve to support or disprove your hypothesis and be great sources of information for your project. A journal article might be too narrowly focused and too detailed for your project. However, you might find some useful information within that article that you will need to extract. Journal articles will help you think about your thesis, and as they help to support or disprove it, they will help you develop your own thoughts and come to your own unique conclusions about your topic.

Besides publishing primary research, journals publish editorials, news items, and reviews. When using a journal to find a scholarly, primary source, be sure you are not using these items. It takes time to produce a research article, gathering information, running an experiment, analyzing the results, and writing the report. The publication process takes more time than a magazine article because each submission must be read and evaluated by a group of peers who need to agree that the article is worthy of publication.

Indexes

Indexes are unique publications. They make it easier to find information. This book has an index that helps you find specific pieces of information within it. Google (http://www.google.com) and Bing (http://www.bing.com) index the Internet to help you find the websites you want. Without indexes, accessing information would be very difficult and time consuming.

Bibliographies are a unique form of index and the first indexes that were developed to help researchers find information across multiple sources. A bibliography is a list of information resources related by topic. The first bibliographies were lists of books because books were the primary method of communicating information. Bibliographies are still around. Your library, no doubt, has a number of bibliographies in its collection. As publishing developed and magazines, journals, and newspapers were published, indexes were developed to help people find information within those publications. Print indexes often indexed the contents of many magazines and journals, and they took up a lot of space in libraries. Finding citations to appropriate information sources in bibliographies and print indexes took a lot of time. With the development of computers came the development of electronic indexes and our databases of today. Databases allow us to search in minutes what used to take many hours to do.

Databases have a very broad scope; even databases that are narrowly focused try to index the entire contents of many information resources, although their depth varies. Print indexes and bibliographies are shallow. They give you enough information to find the original source, the citation information, and sometimes they give you a short summary, called an abstract and/or a critical comment about the information source, called an annotation. Databases have these same features, and they can also have the full text of the information source, which gives them tremendous depth as well. These are full-text databases. Some databases contain citation and abstract information only, while other databases are a hybrid, containing full-text information for some of their sources and citation/abstract information only from other information sources.

Indexes have to be published after the sources they index are published. For databases, that publication happens shortly after the sources' publication. For example, *ProQuest Newspapers*, which is a database of newspapers, will update or publish new entries for the articles within the *Chicago Tribune* just hours after the paper is published!

Not every database is updated this quickly, but they generally have a short time to publication. We talk more about databases in chapter 3.

Vocabulary

books	news sources
current information	popular information
historical information	primary information
indexes	publishing
information access	reference sources
information need	research question
information process	scholarly information
journals	secondary information
magazines	time to publication

Questions

What is an information need?

How do you refine your research question?

What are the three broad categories of knowledge?

What is the information process?

What are the differences between primary and secondary information?

What are the definitions of the different types of information sources?

What is "time to publication," and how does it impact the information you find?

Assignment

Take your three topics from chapter 1, assign them to their category of knowledge, then pick one of the three topics and list at least five different concepts or aspects of your topic. Finally, use your topic and key concepts to help you generate a research question. See the example in Figure 2.3.

TOPIC IDEAS	BRANCH OF KNOWLEDGE	TOPIC	ASPECTS OF TOPIC
1. Climate change 2. Illegal drugs 3. Eating disorders	1. Science 2. Social Science 3. Science	Climate change	1. Ocean temperatures 2. Marine mammals 3. Rising sea levels 4. Climate refuges 5. Economic impact
Research Question What impact has climate change had on marine mammal populations?			

Figure 2.3: Topic and Aspects Worksheet.

CHAPTER 3

Finding Information

You will be searching databases to find the information you need to answer your research question. In this chapter, we will talk about databases and how to find the information you need quickly and effectively. Your library has access to a number of different databases. First, we need to establish what a database is.

What Is a Database?

A *database* is a collection of records. A *record* is a collection of fields. A *field* is a container for specific information. That definition, while technically accurate, may not be the most helpful. Figure 3.1 is an illustration of a single record taken from the NLM Gateway database (http://gateway.nlm.nih.gov).

The first field in the record is the title of the article, "Effect of sugar-free Red Bull . . . " Every record in the database has an article title field that specifically and only contains the title of the article. The names of the authors are put in the author field, the abstract goes in the abstract field, and so forth. This database does not contain the full text of the article. If it did, there would be another field, a very big one, that contained the whole text of the article. Every record in the database has all of these fields. A database can have only a few records or millions of records.

Some words in a database are not searchable. These words are called *stop words*. Stop words are usually short and very common words like "the," "a," "an," "was," and "to." Other stop words are words that have a special meaning to the database and are used in searching like the Boolean operators, And, Or, and Not. You do not need to capitalize the

Field Names	Record
Article Title:	Effect of sugar-free Red Bull energy drink on high-intensity run time-to-exhaustion in young adults.
Authors:	Candow DG, Kleisinger AK, Grenier S, Dorsch KD.
Journal Name:	*J Strength Cond Res*. 2009 Jul;23(4):1271-5.
Contact Info:	Faculty of Kinesiology and Health Studies, University of Regina, Regina, Saskatchewan, Canada. darren.candow@uregina.ca
Abstract:	Consuming sugar-free Red Bull energy drink before exercise has become increasingly popular among exercising individuals. The main purported active ingredient in sugar-free Red Bull is caffeine, which has been shown to increase aerobic exercise performance. The purpose of this study was to determine the effects of sugar-free Red Bull energy drink on high-intensity run time-to-exhaustion in young adults. [...] There were no differences in run time-to-exhaustion (Red Bull: 12.6 +/- 3.8 minutes, placebo: 11.8 +/- 3.4 minutes), perceived exertion (Red Bull: 17.1 +/- 2.0, placebo: 16.6 +/- 1.8), or blood lactate between groups. In conclusion, sugar-free Red Bull energy drink did not influence high-intensity run time-to-exhaustion in young adults.

Subject Terms:	MeSH Terms:
	    Analysis of Variance
	    *Beverages
	    Caffeine/*pharmacology
	    Central Nervous System Stimulants/*pharmacology [...]
	    Young Adult

Article ID Number: PMID: 19528841 [PubMed - indexed for MEDLINE]

Figure 3.1: Record from a Database.

operators when using them in your searches. They are capitalized here for illustrative purposes.

Databases allow you to search quickly through large amounts of information for multiple terms, and the database will retrieve only those articles with the combination of words that you specified. Additionally, each field in a database can be searched individually or in combination with other fields. This makes it easy to find articles written by a specific author or that use a specific subject term. Knowing how a database is structured and searched will help you find the information you need quickly.

Free Databases

Databases fall into two broad categories: free and fee. Google and Bing are examples of free databases. You do not pay to use them, and most importantly, they try to index the entire visible Web. When you do a Google search, you can find information on websites that are open for everyone to access. This is the visible Web. The information you find on the visible Web can be great or horrible. Because anyone can create and post information to the Web, it is important to evaluate the information you find. We will talk about how to do that in chapter 4.

A more scholarly example of a free database is Directory of Open Access Journals (DOAJ) (http://www.doaj.org/doaj). The DOAJ indexes free or open access journals. These are scholarly, peer reviewed publications that are made available free of charge on the Internet. By using DOAJ, you are limiting the amount of information you will find versus a Bing or Google search, but you are getting an assurance of quality.

Fee Databases

Fee databases or commercial databases charge you to use their resources. Fee databases are part of the invisible Web. They cannot be accessed by everyone, and the information they contain may not be found with a Web search. This is what makes them invisible on the Web. The information they contain comes from news sources, magazines, journals, books, and reference sources. Most of the resources in fee databases come from commercial publishers and are collected by commercial database vendors. Both of these entities have a profit motive. They want to make money off of the information they have produced and packaged. Publishers charge database vendors to use their materials. Database vendors charge users for aggregating information from many sources and for providing a search mechanism to find the information. For example, you can buy a copy of *Rolling Stone* at the store, or you can read it on *Academic Search Premier*, a database that includes the full text of many magazines and journals put together by the company EBSCOhost. But no matter how you want to use it, you will have to pay for it. Fortunately, libraries buy these resources and make them available to you at no cost. Even though these resources come from commercial publishers and cost somebody money, you still need to evaluate the information you get from them.

Searching Databases

It is easy to search a database. Type something in the search box, hit Enter, and you should find some information. Searching a database well takes more skill. When you search a database, the records it finds are your search results, and these records, often displayed in a shortened form, are called the results list.

When you search a database for a broad topic, such as "climate change," the database will retrieve many records. Your results list will be very long, and your retrieval will be high. However, the relevance of the material to your research question could be low. Even though you found many items, they are not all what you are looking for, and you will have to look through lots of records to find the good ones.

Retrieval is simply how many items you find, and relevance is how appropriate those items are for your research. If you do a very specific search and find only a few articles, the retrieval is low, but all the information could be appropriate for your topic, so the relevance is high, but you may not have enough information. You want to find a balance between retrieval and relevance. Knowing how to search databases will help you strike this balance and find the information you need efficiently and effectively.

Basic Search

The Google/Bing search box is an example of a basic search. Commercial databases and library catalogs have basic search screens as well. You type words into the search box, and the database searches multiple fields to find matches. The words you entered are your search terms. It is a very simple way to conduct a search, but not necessarily the best. It is a quick way to get an idea about how much information is available on your topic, but the basic search is making the decisions for you about where it looks for your search terms and how they are combined (see Figure 3.2).

Advanced Search

The advanced search screens give you control over how your search is carried out. You can pick the specific fields you want to search and easily specify how you want to combine your search terms. When you use the advanced search screen, it is easier to understand what the search is doing, which also makes it easier to modify your search to change the number of results you receive (see Figure 3.3).

Figure 3.2: Basic Search Screen.

Figure 3.3: Advanced Search Screen.

Language of the Search

You can search databases with either keywords or specific subject terms. This is the language of the search.

Keyword Searching and Synonyms

Keywords are the words and phrases that best describe your topic. Keywords are your own words. They are the words that you thought of when you developed your topic and research question. Take your keywords from your research question. These are the words you want to search to find information that matches your research question.

Not all words in your research question make good keywords. See the example in Figure 3.4. Why is "impact" not a keyword? It is not an essential descriptor of your topic. You cannot search for your topic without "ocean temperatures," "whales," and "population," but you can search for it without "impact." If you use "impact" in your search, you will miss all the article that use the words "influence," "effect," and "bearing" instead. So using the word "impact" limits your search, but not to an aspect of your topic, just to that word. "Impact" is a verb in our research question. Nouns make better search terms than verbs.

Keyword is the default search. The search will look for your term in any field in the database and return only the records that have your keyword in one or more of the fields. It is important to choose good keywords. If your keyword is not a good way to describe your topic, you will not find the information you need. Thinking of synonyms for your keywords will help your search.

Synonyms are words that mean the same thing. When it comes to database searching, that definition is a little narrow. For database searching, a synonym may be a similar or related topic. You need to think of synonyms when you are preparing to search databases.

TOPIC	ASPECTS OF TOPIC	RESEARCH QUESTION	KEYWORDS
Climate change	Rising sea levels. Climate refugees. Marine life. Food production. Rising ocean temperatures. Erratic weather.	How will rising ocean temperatures impact whale habitats and populations?	ocean temperatures
			habitat
			population
			whales

Figure 3.4: Keyword Worksheet.

TOPIC	ASPECTS OF TOPIC	RESEARCH QUESTION	KEYWORDS AND SYNONYMS
Climate change	Rising sea levels. Climate refugees. Marine life. Food production. Rising ocean temperatures. Erratic weather.	How will rising ocean temperatures impact whale habitats and populations?	ocean temperatures water temperatures sea temperatures
			habitat behavior range
			population reproduction numbers
			whales marine mammals dolphins cetaceans seals

Figure 3.5: Synonym Worksheet.

Synonyms will help you broaden your search and increase the amount of material you find. Synonyms might turn out to be better search terms than your original keywords (see Figure 3.5).

Subject Searching and Field Searching

Subject searching is using specific language to search the subject field of a database. That language is called *controlled vocabulary* because a specific subject term is assigned to all articles on the same topic. For example, if you want to find all the articles in a database that mention teens in association with the rest of your topic, you would need to use your synonyms and search for "teens," "teenagers," "youths," "minors," and "adolescents." However, if you knew that the database assigned the term "adolescents" to every article that mentions teens, teenagers, or any of the other variations, you could search only one term and search it in the subject field to find all the articles.

The vocabulary is controlled by the company that puts together the database. They have employees examine the articles they are going to include in their database and assign subject headings to each article from a list of approved terms. The list is called a thesaurus. This step ensures that all articles on the same topic are described in the same way, and that makes subject searching a very effective way to find information.

When you limit your search to a specific field within a database, you are performing a field search. Subject searching is a specific type of field searching. You can also limit your search to any other field in a database. For example, if you know the author of an article or book you want to find, you can search for their name in the author field. This narrows the focus of your search. The name is only searched in the author field, not in the rest of the fields. This means that even if you search a common name like Williams, you are only finding Williams as an author, not as a subject or as a word in the title.

Another useful field search is the title search. If you know the title, using a title search will often find exactly the information you want. Limiting your keywords to the title field is a way to narrow your search and find fewer results. It can be a very helpful way to retrieve more relevant items. Then you can examine those records to find official subject terms, and if you need to find more items, search those subject terms to find additional relevant items.

Mechanics of the Search

Databases use commands to combine your search terms and execute a search. These commands are the search language of the database, as opposed to keywords, which are the language used in the search. When you put together these commands with your keywords, you create a search statement. Using keywords from our example in Figure 3.4, if you search for "whales," then you have a very simple search statement that does not need any command, but you get too much information. If you want to search for "whales," "ocean temperatures," and "population," you need to combine these terms using the proper commands to get the information you want. Understanding search mechanics and commands will enable you to get it right.

Boolean Operators

One very important set of commands are the Boolean operators. Boolean operators were developed by George Boole, an English mathematician in the 19th century (Gillispie 1970). The operators are

- And
- Or
- Not

Boolean operators are used to control how your keywords and subject terms are combined in a search statement. Boolean opera-

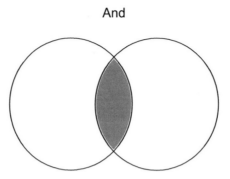

And

Figure 3.6: And Operator.

tors are used in all commercial databases. The And operator finds the intersection of your ideas. It narrows your search, giving you fewer, more relevant results. In other words, it increases your relevance while decreasing your retrieval. We use Venn diagrams to illustrate how Boolean operators work. Figure 3.6 is a Venn diagram that illustrates how the And operator works with two keywords. The gray area in the middle is where our two ideas overlap or intersect. This area represents the records in the database that mention both of our search terms, and these are the only records that will be retrieved.

In the previous example, assume we searched for "earthquakes and tsunamis." There are 100 articles in our database on earthquakes. There are 100 articles on tsunamis. However, there are only 20 articles that mention both earthquakes and tsunamis. Our search finds only those 20 articles. Where the two circles overlap in the Venn diagram represents those 20 articles that mention both of our keywords.

If we want the intersection of three terms, "earthquakes," "tsunamis," and "models," our search statement should look like this:

- earthquakes and tsunamis and models

The Venn diagram for this search is illustrated in Figure 3.7.

The And operator is very powerful because it brings your ideas together, which is exactly what you want to do to find information that addresses your research question. You can construct excellent searches using only And.

The Boolean operator Or finds the union of ideas. When you join keywords with Or, you find every instance of each of those concepts. The Or operator broadens your search, retrieving more results while

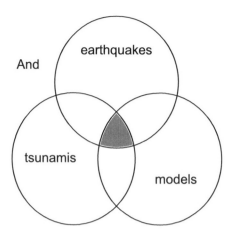

Figure 3.7: Earthquakes and Tsunamis and Models.

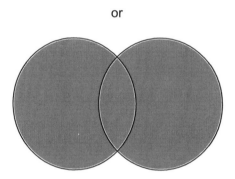

Figure 3.8: Or Operator.

decreasing relevance. Using the terms "earthquakes" and "tsunami" used previously, our search is

■ earthquakes or tsunamis

There are 100 articles about earthquakes and 100 articles about tsunamis in our database and just like the example for And, 20 of those articles mention both. How many total articles did we find? We found 100 + 100–20 or 180 articles that mention either earthquakes or tsunamis. The Venn diagram in Figure 3.8 illustrates how Or works.

The Or operator should be used to group your synonyms together. For example, the synonyms for earthquakes are "tremors," "seismic activity," and "temblors." You can combine all of these synonyms into a set with the search statement

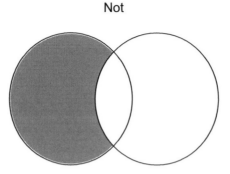

Not

Figure 3.9: Not Operator.

- earthquakes or tremors or seismic activity or temblors

The following section on nesting will explain how to do this and why it is important.

The last Boolean operator is Not. Use the Not operator to exclude ideas from your search, narrowing your results and increasing relevance. For example, if you want to find articles on tsunamis that do not mention earthquakes, your search would be

- tsunamis not earthquakes

With 100 articles about tsunamis and 100 articles about earthquakes and 20 articles that mention both, our search would find the 80 articles that mention only tsunamis, 100–20. Figure 3.9 is the Venn diagram for Not.

The Not operator is the most difficult of the Boolean operators to use, and it has less application than the others as well. You may never need to use the Not operator. It can be useful to exclude ideas that are not the focus of your research or ideas that add ambiguity to your search, although you also run the risk of losing relevant results.

Proximity and Phrase Searching

Proximity searching is a very specific type of And searching that requires your search terms to be close to each other. Unlike the Boolean operators, proximity operators are not standardized and will be different in different databases. You will need to consult the help screens of the database you are searching to find out what the proximity operators are. We will use N/# and W/# as examples of proximity operators. In our example, N/# means that your terms need to be within the specified number of words of each other and in no particular order. Here is a sample search statement:

■ methane n/5 cattle

This search means that the word "methane" must be within five words of "cattle." There is no order implied, so methane can come before or after cattle. W/# has the same meaning with one addition. The words must be in the order specified by the search statement.

■ legalization w/2 drugs

In this example, *legalization* needs to be within two words of *drugs*, but *legalization* must come first.

The double quotation marks are another form of proximity operator. They mean that the words within the quotation marks should be matched in order with the words appearing right next to each other or more simply put, an exact match. This is called *phrase searching*. The double quotation marks as the phrase search operator are supported by most database search engines and even Web search engines like Google. "Climate change," "income tax," "Shakespearian sonnet," and "special interest groups" are all examples of phrases. Enclosing them in quotes ensures that they will be searched for as a phrase and matched exactly. Phrase searching is the most useful and easiest to use of the proximity search, but also the most limiting.

Using proximity in your search statement will result in lower retrieval and higher relevance than even an And search will yield. You should use phrase searching whenever you have two or more words that represent one concept or idea. This will focus your search on that concept and not on the words that make up that concept. It is much better to search for "special interest groups" than to search for *special and interest and groups*.

Nesting

Nesting is used to group synonyms and control the order of execution in your search statement. The search engines of databases follow rules that define the order of execution of their commands. Typically, And is executed first, then Not, and finally Or. Order of execution impacts your search results, and you need to know how this works in order to get the results you want. For example, your research topic is the impact of climate change on whales. You developed a Boolean search statement complete with synonyms that looks like this:

- "climate change" or "global warming" and whales or cetaceans

You know exactly what you want the database search to find, but the search engine sees your search statement very differently than you do. This is what it sees:

- ("global warming" and whales) or "climate change" or cetaceans

In other words, your search is going to find all the articles that mention both global warming and whales, then it will add those articles to all the articles that mention climate change, then add that to all the articles that mention cetaceans. That is not what you want. The search you want looks like this:

- ("climate change" or "global warming") and (whales or cetaceans)

The parentheses control the order of execution. They tell the database that their portion of the search needs to be done first. In this case, the search engine would execute the search for "climate change or global warming" first. It will hold these results as a set, then look for "whales or cetaceans" and create a set from that information. Finally it will And those two sets of information together to achieve the results you want.

Truncation and Wildcards

Web search engines are powerful pieces of software that automatically search for other forms of the words you enter in your search. If you search for "computer," you will also get results for "computers." Commercial databases are not as sophisticated, yet. They search for exactly what you enter. To find forms of a word, you need to include them all in your search. For example, if you are looking for articles on computers, you would want to search for

- (computer or computers)

This would find both the singular and plural forms of the word.

Commercial databases do make it a little easier by supporting truncation. Truncation allows you to find various word endings with a single search term. Truncation broadens your search results, increases your retrieval, and decreases your relevance because truncation is an Or operator. With truncation, our previous example would simply be

- computer*

This will find both "computer" and "computers" and any other words you can make by adding letters to "computer" like "computerized." If our truncation was like this

- comput*

Then the search would find these words: computation, computations, compute, computed, computes, computer, computers, computing, and so forth.

The rest of your search statement will give the truncation context, which will help eliminate the forms of the word that you do not want. However, you need to be careful with truncation. If you shorten a word dramatically, it will find too many other words and hurt your search.

In some cases, it is best not to truncate. For example, if you are looking for articles on cats, it is best to search for (cat or cats) and not cat*. There are too many possible word endings that can be attached to "cat", and your search results will not be what you expected.

The asterisk is often the symbol used for the truncation operator. However, there are some databases that use different symbols. If your search does not seem to be giving you the results you expect when you truncate, then you may need to consult the help screens to see what the truncation symbol is.

Wildcards are used to find variant spellings within a word. If you are searching for articles on the use of color by the Navajo, your search may look like this:

- colo?r and Nava?o

This search statement will find both the English and British spelling of color and the variant spelling of Navajo. Here is the search using the Or operator instead of wildcards:

- (color or colour) and (Navajo or Navaho)

The wildcard operator varies from database to database. Some databases may even have a number of wildcard operators that have slightly different functions. You will need to consult the help screens to find out what the operators are for the database you are searching. Wildcards are not needed nearly as often as truncation, but they can save you some time and complexity in your search when you do need them.

Using Help Screens

Help screens are available in most databases. Often, there is a link to "Help" in the upper right corner of the page, but you may have to look around to find the link. Help screens provide information on how to search the database, fields, and operators that are available; any special features or searches that you can use; and viewing and saving your results. If you are unsure about a search you are performing, a quick look at the help screens may answer your questions.

Refining the Search

When you search a database, chances are your first search will not be perfect. It will retrieve either too many or too few items. Knowing how a search works allows you to quickly refine your search. In the sample worksheet in Figure 3.10 we have entered a search that found too few items. To use the worksheet, you Or together all the words in one row, then you And together each of the rows. This worksheet is based on the advanced search screens you will see in a number of databases and represents the way you should use the advanced search screen.

		KEYWORD	OR	SYNONYM 1	OR	SYNONYM 2
	1st concept	climate change				
And	2nd concept	whale*				
And	3rd concept	population*				
Search Statement "climate change" and whale* and population*						

Figure 3.10: Search Worksheet with Search Strategy.

		KEYWORD	OR	SYNONYM 1	OR	SYNONYM 2
	1st concept	climate change	or	global warming		
And	2nd concept	whale*	or	cetacean*	or	marine mammal*
And	3rd concept	population*	or	reproduction	or	number*
~~And~~	~~4th concept~~	~~habitat*~~				
Search Statement ("climate change" or "global warming") and (whale* or cetacean* or "marine mammal*") and (population or reproduction)						

Figure 3.11: Search Worksheet with Broadened Search Strategy.

The search in this worksheet would look like this:

- "climate change" and whale* and population* and habitat*

Here are the changes you can make to broaden this search. First, you can delete a row, which removes one of the And operators. With one less intersection of ideas, the search will return more items. Second, you can use Or operators to add synonyms to your search, which will also retrieve more items. Finally, you can do both. In the example in Figure 3.11 the possible additions you can make to broaden your search have a gray background. The possible deletion you can make to broaden your search has a strikethrough.

If your search finds too many items, then you will want to narrow your search. Narrowing your search gives you a chance to focus on a more specific aspect of your topic or add another concept to your search. To narrow your search, you can add a row to the search worksheet with an And operator. This will narrow your results by requiring another intersection of ideas. You can also remove your synonyms and Or operators, or you can use a combination of both techniques. In the example in Figure 3.12 the possible additions have a gray background, and the possible deletions have a strikethrough.

Refining your search to get better results is quick and easy to do when you know how databases work. Refining your search may also help you focus in on a specific aspect of your topic or even change your research question altogether as you find articles that hold more interest for you.

		KEYWORD	OR	SYNONYM 1	OR	SYNONYM 2
	1st concept	climate change	or	~~global warming~~		
And	2nd concept	~~whale*~~	or	~~cetacean*~~	or	marine mammal*
And	3rd concept	population*	or	~~reproduction~~	or	~~number*~~
And	4th concept	habitat*	or	~~behavior~~		
Search Statement "climate change" and "marine mammal*" and population* and habitat*							

Figure 3.12: Search Worksheet with Narrowed Search Strategy.

Vocabulary

" "

( )

advanced search

and operator

basic search

Boolean operators

controlled vocabulary

database

field searching

fields in a database

index in a database

invisible Web

keywords

nesting

not operator

or operator

phrase

proximity

records in a database

relevance

retrieval

search statement

search terms

stop words

subject searching

synonyms

truncation

Venn diagrams

visible Web

Questions

What is the difference between free and fee databases?

What is the difference between a basic search and an advanced search?

What do each of the Boolean operators do?

What is a search statement?

How do double quotation marks work in a search?

What is truncation?

What do parentheses do in a search?

Assignment

Take your research question from chapter 2, pull out the keywords, and enter them on a search worksheet. Then think of synonyms for each of your keywords. Finally, write a Boolean search statement using truncation where appropriate with the information entered into your search worksheet. See the example in Figure 3.13.

		KEYWORD	OR	SYNONYM 1	OR	SYNONYM 2
Research Question What impact has climate change had on marine mammal populations and behaviors?						
	1st concept	climate change	or	global warming		
And	2nd concept	whale*	or	cetacean*	or	marine mammal*
And	3rd concept	population	or	reproduction		
Search Statement ("climate change" or "global warming") and (whale* or cetacean* or "marine mammal*") and (population or reproduction)						

Figure 3.13: Search Statement Worksheet.

CHAPTER 4

Utilizing the Library Catalog and Resources

Your library's home page will guide you to all the resources the library owns and can access. Somewhere on your library's home page you will find access to the library catalog. The catalog lists all the materials that the library owns in print and electronic formats. Through the catalog, you will find books that your library has shelved in the stacks, eBooks, and eReference books that you can access directly from their catalog records. Catalogs also list the titles of journals that your library owns in print. However to access the contents of the journals in order to find articles on a particular topic, you will need to use the other databases that your library provides. We will look at those databases in chapter 5.

Searching the Library Catalog

It is likely that your library's catalog is the smallest database that your library has access to. It may consist of only 10,000 or 100,000 items. While that does not sound very small, compared to the commercial databases and the Web, it is small. When you search a small database, you will need to broaden your search to find relevant material. If you want to find reference material in the library catalog, you will have to think in very broad terms about your topic and craft a search statement accordingly.

There are many different software options for library catalogs. Your public library catalog may be very different from the catalog you use at school. However, all catalogs support keyword Boolean searches. Library catalogs make it easy to do field searching because searching for a title, an author or a subject is common in a library catalog. If you want to see if your library owns a specific book, then a title search is fast and efficient. If you are looking for books by a certain author, then the author search is a better search than a keyword search.

Subject searching, as discussed in chapter 3, is a little more difficult. You will not know the official subject terms until you try a keyword search and find relevant records whose subject terms you can check. However, there is a specific subset of subject searching that comes up often when searching the catalog. For example, if you want to find books *about* Ansel Adams as opposed to books *by* Ansel Adams, then a subject search is the best approach because it will focus only on the books *about* him and not include the books *by* him.

Library catalogs often have special searches that let you browse through records. You can browse by author, title, subject, and call number. These searches will show you a list of results based on your search. If you do a browse search of Adams as an author, you will get a list of all the Adamses who have written a book that your library has purchased. Often, this results list will show how many books your library has for each author. If you are unsure of the spelling of an author's name or do not know their first name, if you want to see how many items your library has in a given subject, or if you want to see what is on the shelf in a specific area, these searches are very helpful.

Your library's catalog may have other features that are designed to make using the library easier for you. The catalog may allow you to see what you have checked out and allow you to renew those items with a click of the mouse. It may allow you to place holds on items that are checked out so that you will be contacted as soon as that item is returned. It may let you keep lists of items you want to read. Be sure to explore your catalog and see what features it has to offer.

Retrieving Materials

If the material you find is print, then you will need to copy down the call number, which is a unique identifying number, and find the item on the shelf. The catalog should also tell you what collection the item is in. It could be in the circulating collection, the collection of books that you can check out, or it could be in the DVD collection, or it could be in the reference collection. Books in the reference collection cannot be checked out. However, they are often designed for quick use, which you can do in the library.

Your library will have the books shelved by either Dewey Decimal Classification call numbers or Library of Congress Classification call numbers. Both systems are designed to place items on the shelf by subject so that items on the same subject are filed next to each other. This makes it easy to browse the shelves and find other items on your topic. The Dewey Decimal Classification is often used in smaller libraries, public libraries, and schools libraries. The Library of Congress Classification system is designed for larger libraries. You will find it in use at most large public and academic libraries.

The Dewey Decimal Classification divides knowledge into 10 broad areas from 000 to 900. For example, the 100s are philosophy and psychology, the 300s are social sciences, and the 700s are arts and recreation. Within each area there are many subcategories. For example, 770 is the number for photography. 778.9 is the number for nature photography.

Items are arranged on the shelves from low numbers to high numbers. Dewey makes that easy to understand. It is a decimal system, however, and confusion can arise from the numbers following the decimal point. The following sequence of decimal numbers is in order from smallest to largest.

- .1, .11, .12, .125, .13, .17, .2

For example, if your library had books with the numbers 800.125 and 800.2, the book numbered 800.125 would come first because it is the smaller number.

Library of Congress call numbers use letters and numbers to designate subjects. The broad categories include A for general works, B for philosophy, psychology, and religion, then skipping ahead, H is for social science and business, L is for education, P is language and literature, T is science, and so on. For a complete list of the Library of Congress classification you can look at the Wikipedia article (Library of Congress Classification 2011).

A second letter is used to divide the topics into smaller categories, and then numbers on a second line divide those categories into even smaller subject categories. For example, B is the broad category for philosophy, psychology, and religion. BF 1 to BF 990 is the category for psychology, with BF 173–175.5 for psychoanalysis, BF176–176.5

DEWEY DECIMAL NUMBER	LIBRARY OF CONGRESS CALL NUMBER
523.2	QB
.S63	601
2005	.S63
	2005

Figure 4.1: Dewey Decimal and Library of Congress Call Number for *The Planets*.

for psychological tests and testing, BF180–198.7 for experimental psychology, and so forth. Library of Congress call numbers usually have the letters on one line and the numbers on the second line. Those numbers are decimal numbers, just like in the Dewey system, which means a book with the call number BF 181.41 would come before a book with the call number BF 181.5.

Both Dewey and Library of Congress use Cutter numbers and year of publication to further identify a specific book. A Cutter number is frequently based on the author's name. If there is no author, then the Cutter number is based on the title of the book. The first element of a Cutter number is the first letter of the author's last name, then numbers are assigned to the second, third, and maybe fourth letters of the author's name. Cutter numbers are decimal numbers, so a book with a Cutter number of .C583 would come before a book with a Cutter number of .C59, if the rest of the call number was the same. The year of publication will distinguish different editions of a book from each other. A book with a year of publication of 2005 would be shelved before a book with a year of publication of 2011, if the rest of the call number was the same. Figure 4.1 is an example of a Dewey Decimal number and a Library of Congress number for the same book, *The Planets* by Dava Sobel, which includes both a Cutter number and the year of publication.

Utilizing Print Sources

Once you have found the items you need on the shelf, you need to find the information you want within the source. Just as you are not going to read an entire reference book to find the few pieces of information that you need, you also may not need to read a whole circulating book, but only the chapter that relates to your research question. To get at the information contained within these sources quickly, you need to take advantage of the options they give you.

Reference sources are designed for the quick look up of information and are most frequently arranged alphabetically, making them easy to use. If you cannot find the information you need, be sure to check the index located at the back of the book. What you are looking for may not have its own entry, but it may be part of another entry. The index of any book will guide you to the entry or chapter where that term is mentioned. Use the table of contents to find a chapter or section of a book that relates to your research question.

When you are reading from a source be sure to take notes and summarize the information you find. If you come across a particular sentence or phrase that you really like, copy it verbatim so you can quote it in your research paper. You should note the page number where you found the quote, and always copy the citation information for your source. You will need this information for your in-text citations and your bibliography.

How you take your notes and record citation information is up to you. You can use pen and paper or programs like OneNote, Evernote (http://www.evernote.com), Microsoft Word, or OpenOffice.org Writer (http://www.openoffice.org) for your note taking and programs like EasyBib (http://www.easybib.com), EndNote (http://www.endnote.com), or Zotero (http://www.zotero.org) for your bibliography. What is important is that you record your quotes and citation information accurately. We discuss this subject more in chapter 11.

Utilizing Electronic Sources

You may find eBooks and eReference books on your results list when you search your library's catalog. These sources have the same features of their print counterparts. You can use the index or table of contents to find the information you are looking for or browse through their contents. Unlike their print counterparts, these are electronic databases that also support the search functions we talked about in chapter 3. Searching these resources takes you directly to the information you want.

Because these are electronic resources, they have special features that make them easier to use than their print counterparts. We look at these features when we talk about using databases in chapter 5.

Vocabulary

author search	Cutter number
browse search	Dewey Decimal Classification
call number	index

library catalog

Library of Congress call
    numbers

subject search

table of contents

title search

Questions

How is the library catalog different from other databases?

What unique searches can be performed in the library catalog?

How do call numbers work?

How do you find information within a book?

Assignment

Find four books and one reference book that you would consider using in your research on your topic in your library catalog. Sources can be print or electronic. Record the search you used to find the items and the call number, author, and title of each item. See Figure 4.2.

Library Catalog Search Worksheet			
Search Statement for Books global warming and ocean*			
	CALL NUMBER	**TITLE**	**AUTHOR**
1.	QC903 .A73 2010	The climate crisis: an introductory guide to climate change	Archer, David
2.	QC981.8 .C5 K875 2009	Global climate change and the road to extinction: the legal and planning response	Kushner, James A.
3.	GB5014 .S58 2008	Global catastrophes and trends: the next 50 years	Smil, Vaclav
4.	QE721.2 .E97 W384 2007	Under a green sky: global warming, the mass extinctions of the past, and what they mean for our future	Ward, Peter Douglas,
Search Statement for Reference Book global warming			
1.	Online	Encyclopedia of global warming and climate change [electronic resource]	Philander, S. George

Figure 4.2: Library Catalog Worksheet.

Utilizing Library Databases

Your library's home page will direct you to the databases that you can search. While the library catalog list the names of journals that the library subscribes to, these databases give you access to the articles contained within the journals. Your library may have only a handful of databases, or it may have hundreds of databases, and each database may contain tens of thousands or even millions of records. Knowing which one of those databases you should use for your research can be intimidating.

Choosing a Database

Your library will have a general database, one that has information in all subject areas. It may even be highlighted on the library's webpage. This is a good place to start your research. You can try out your search statement; find some relevant articles that will help you identify other, better keywords and subject terms; narrow the focus of your research; and perhaps even find enough good information for your research.

If you do not find enough information in a general database, then you will have to try a subject-specific database. These are databases that focus on a specific field of knowledge or subject discipline. There are databases for every subject area, including biology, literature, psychology, business, and everything else. Your library's webpage probably has a list of databases by subject with a brief description of what is contained within each database. You may have to look around the library's website to find it, but this will help you pick a database.

Your library may also have something called *federated searching*. Federated searching executes your search in multiple databases at the same time. Not all libraries have federated searching, and it may not be called that on your library's webpages. It may be a search box labeled "Find Articles" or "Search for Journal Articles in Multiple Databases." In cases like this, a predetermined subset of the library's databases will be searched. You may also be able to choose other predefined collections of databases to search which are grouped by subject, or you may be able to pick the databases you want to search for yourself.

For federated searching to work with multiple databases from multiple vendors, it can only use the most basic search features. In that regard, federated searching typically supports Boolean operators, phrase searching, and field searching. It does not support proximity operators and special features like user accounts. Federated searching can be confusing to use because of feature differences, how results are displayed, and the large amount of records that it might find. However, you can browse through your results list and find the articles you need. Another way to use federated searching is to do a quick search, and then look at the results to see how many hits your search had in each database that was searched. You can use these results to pick the databases that seem best for your research and search them more thoroughly. Federated searching is another tool that your library has and one that is worth exploring.

Citation, Abstract, and Full-Text Databases

Another thing to be aware of when choosing a database is what kind of information it contains. There are some databases that contain only citations, which is the information needed to find an article, including the author, title of the article, and publication information. There are databases that contain citations and abstracts, and there are databases that contain the full text of every article they index. Citation and abstract databases are not that common anymore. Full-text databases are also not the norm. Most databases are a hybrid. They have full text of articles for some portion of the records in the database and abstracts for the rest.

When you find an article that looks good for your research, but it is not available in full text in the database you searched, there are a few things you can try. First, your library may have something called a "link resolver," which will check the other databases your library has to see if the article you want is available in full text in any of them. Then it will provide you a link to that article in the other databases. The link for the link resolver will be displayed on both the results list under each item record and on the full record display for the individual record. Look for a link that says something like "check other databases" or "find full text."

If the article you want is not available in full text in any of the library's databases, then you will need to check the library's print holdings to see if the library subscribes to paper copies of the journal that contains the article. One way to find this information is to search the library's catalog for the journal title. That will tell you if your library subscribes to the journal and what years it owns. There may be other ways to find this information as well, and if your library does not have the article you want in print or any of its databases, then ask the librarian what your options are. We talk about library services that can help you in these situations in chapter 7.

Hybrid databases allow you to limit your search to the full text content. This is very useful when you do not have much time to get your research done. However, you may miss a good article that, while not full text in the database you searched, is full text in another database your library has. Be careful when selecting full text only searches; you might be missing some good, relevant articles.

Utilizing Electronic Sources

Databases have many features to help you use the information you found. You can print, save, or email an article of interest. There are usually links to these features at the top of the results list or the top of an individual record display. Databases allow you to mark records. This means you select the items that interest you from your results by either checking a box by the records or clicking on a link that says "Add to folder." You can then print, save, or email your entire list at one time by clicking on a "folder" or "marked items" link. This is a very convenient way to work with multiple records. However, it is important to note that when you finish your searching and log out of the database, your marked items disappear. Many databases offer services that will allow you to save your marked items in a personal account so you can return to them later. You need to register for this service, but it is free. This is a great feature and will aid you in your research.

Some databases also have special features like the one mentioned previously that can save your marked records for you. They may also be able to save your search statements and run them automatically to find any new articles that have been added to the database that meet your search criteria, and then inform you of the results through email or a feed to your news reader. Databases can even be set up to contact you with the table of contents for new issues of journals that you read. The special features that databases offer vary by database vendor, but it is worth your time to find out what features are available to you because they will help you with your research.

Of course, full-text databases make it easy to copy and paste quotes into your note taking or word processing software. Doing this ensures that you will have the wording exactly right. Databases also provide citation tools that will help you cite the article you are viewing or all of your marked articles, but not all of the citations generated by the databases are perfectly correct. You will need to check each citation to make sure it is in the proper format. Citations can also be exported to your favorite citation manager program.

When you are reading long articles or book chapters online, you can use the "find" feature of your Internet browser to locate a word or phrase in an HTML document or use the search feature in Reader to find a word in a PDF file. Be sure to take notes and be able to summarize the article. Also, think about how the article does or does not support your research. We talk about how to evaluate the information you found for quality in chapter 8.

Vocabulary

abstract databases	hybrid databases
citation databases	link resolver
federated searching	marked records
full-text databases	print holdings
general database	subject-specific database

Questions

What is the difference between a database that contains abstracts only and a hybrid database?

What is federated searching?

Where is the listing for databases on your library's website?

How do you save or email records?

How do you get an MLA citation for an article from a particular database?

Assignment

Find two newspaper articles, two magazine articles, and four journal articles that you would consider using in your research on your topic in appropriate databases. Record the search you used to find the items and the author, title, and source of each item. See the example in Figure 5.1.

Search Statement for Newspaper Articles			
"global warming" and "marine mammal*" and population			
NEWSPAPER ARTICLES			
	AUTHOR	**TITLE**	**SOURCE**
1.	Lindsey Wiebe	Killer whales benefit from global warming: researchers	*The Ottawa Citizen.* Ottawa, Ont.: Mar 11, 2009. p. A.2
2.	DAN JOLING	Humpback, fin whales noted in Arctic Ocean ; OUT OF USUAL RANGE	The Associated Press. *Anchorage Daily News.* Anchorage, Alaska: Nov 8, 2007. p. B.1
Search Statement for Magazine Articles			
"global warming" and whale* and population			
MAGAZINE ARTICLES			
1.	MacDonald, Nancy	AN OCEAN OF POISON	*Maclean's,* 8/3/2009, Vol. 122 Issue 29/30, p. 36–37
2.	Drew, Lisa W	BERING SEA BLUES	Feb/Mar2008, Vol. 46 Issue 2, p. 22-30
Search Statement for Journal Articles			
("global warming" or "climate change") and whale*			
JOURNAL ARTICLES			
1.	HEIDE-JØRGENSEN, M. P.; LAIDRE, K. L.; BURT, M. L.; BORCHERS, D. L.; MARQUES, T. A.; HANSEN, R. G.; RASMUSSEN, M.; FOSSETTE, S.	Abundance of narwhals (Monodon monoceros) on the hunting grounds in Greenland	*Journal of Mammalogy,* Oct 2010, Vol. 91 Issue 5, p. 1135–1151

Figure 5.1: Database Search Worksheet.

2.	Lambert, Emily; Hunter, Colin; Pierce, Graham J.; MacLeod, Colin D.	Sustainable whale-watching tour-ism and climate change: towards a framework of resilience	*Journal of Sustainable Tourism,* Apr 2010, Vol. 18 Issue 3, p. 409–427
3.	Rieser, Alison	WHALES, WHALING, AND THE WARMING OCEANS	*Boston College Environmental Affairs Law Review,* 2009, Vol. 36 Issue 2, p. 401–429
4.	Whitehead, Hal; McGill, Brian; Worm, Boris	Diversity of deep-water cetaceans in relation to temperature: implications for ocean warming	*Ecology Letters,* Nov 2008, Vol. 11 Issue 11, p. 1198–1207

Figure 5.1: (*Continued*)

CHAPTER 6

Utilizing the Web

There is a lot of good information, and there is a lot of bad information available to everyone on the Internet. Internet search engines such as Bing and Google are easy to use and work well. Did you know that both of these search engines have advanced search screens that allow you to limit your search to a specific domain, and that there are search services that will execute your search in multiple search engines at the same time?

Web Search Engines

We are all familiar with the simple search box that Internet search engines present us. A lot of technology hides behind that search box to help you find the two or three good webpages on a topic out of the 38 billion pages that Google indexes (de Kunder 2011).

Basic Searching

The basic search in an Internet search engine will use an implied Boolean And operator between your search terms. For example, if you entered

- global warming whales population

The search engine will look for

- global and warming and whales and population

The implied And operator is necessary because the size of the index is so large. Even with this feature, our original search of these terms retrieves 3.29 million hits.

Phrase searching using the double quotation marks is supported by Internet search engines. Our search would be better if it looked like this:

- "global warming" whales population

Phrase searching is an essential tool to use when searching the Internet because of the vast amount of information available. Use phrase searching whenever it is appropriate to help narrow your search results. It is not necessary to use truncation when searching with Internet search engines. They automatically look for variant forms of the words you enter in your search statement.

To make these search results manageable, Internet search engines use algorithms to develop a relevancy ranking for each page. The algorithm counts how many times your search terms appeared in each page and where they appeared on the page, like in the title or in headings. The algorithm also checks to see how many other pages link to the page it is ranking. All this information is assigned a value, added up, and then the page is given a relevancy ranking. The items that are the most relevant to your search appear at the top of the list. This means that they mention your search terms more often, in more prominent places, and are linked to more frequently by other webpages. Relevancy ranking is what makes a results list of three million items meaningful and useful.

You should be aware, however, that the first few hits on the list are probably commercial sites that paid to be there. Also, there are plenty of smart programmers and web designers who know what to do to their websites to improve their relevancy rankings. Remember that while relevancy ranking is a great help, it is not a guarantee that the top few sites have good, reliable information. You still need to evaluate the information you find. We talk about how to do this later in the book.

Advanced Searching

Internet search engines have advanced search screens that, like commercial databases, offer you additional methods to find the information you want. Google and Bing require you to execute a search first, and then they provide a link to the advanced screen where you can modify your search or apply limiters. *Limiters* are additions you can make to your search that do not change your search statement but instead add special conditions that your search needs to meet. The process is called *limiting*. In the library catalog, you can limit your results to a specific collection in the library, a language, a type of media, and year of publication. Internet search engines let you limit your search by language, by file format, and to specific domains, like .edu, .gov, or .com. If you need to find an Excel file, limiting by file format gets rid of all of the other material and just returns Excel files. Limiting your search to the domain .edu finds pages on college and university websites, and .gov limits the search to government websites in the United States. The .com domain used to mean commercial enterprises, and .org used to mean not-for-profit groups, but those definitions no longer apply, and anyone can have a .com or .org website. Be aware of this when limiting your searches by domain.

You can modify your search by requiring terms to be present, an exact phrase to be matched, any of your terms to be present, and by excluding terms from your search. This should sound familiar. This is the search engine equivalent of And, phrase, Or, and Not searching. Google will allow you to specify where your terms are located in the pages it finds, either in the title, the text, the URL, or the default, which is anywhere. This is similar to field searching in commercial databases; however, because webpages do not conform to record formats of commercial databases, there are far fewer fields that can be searched.

The advanced search shows you how your search is being constructed as you fill in the form. For example, if we enter *whales* and *population* into the "must be present" box and *global warming* into the "exact phrase" box, then limit our search to PDF files that are located on educational sites (.edu), our search statement would look like this:

- whale population "global warming" filetype:pdf site:.edu

You can see the commands that are being used to apply limiters to your search with "filetype:" followed by the file extension and "site:" followed by the domain. Knowing this, you can also use these limits in the basic search and not have to go to the advanced search screen.

Metasearch Engines

Metasearch engines execute your search statement in more than one Internet search engine at a time. Dogpile (http://www.dogpile.com) is an example of a metasearch engine. You can use your favorite search engine to find other metasearch engines. The principle behind metasearch engines is the same as federated searching of library databases. If searching one database is good, then searching multiple databases is better. Even though Google searches a massive number of webpages, it does not search all of the same pages that Bing and Yahoo (http://www.yahoo.com) search. Therefore, using a metasearch engine will return the results that each would miss alone. Of course, this could lead to too much information. How a metasearch engine chooses to display the results it finds becomes a very important part of its usability, and you should try a few to find which one you like best.

Utilizing Web Sources

Finding the information you need from within the webpages that you found with your search is easy. You can read the pages or save them on any storage device. You can bookmark them and return to them at any time. You can use the find feature to locate a word or phrase within the page. It is easy to copy and paste portions you want to quote into your word processor, but individual webpages do not offer features that help you cite them, and finding all the information you need to properly cite the webpage may take some looking around. Citation managers are programs that can help you with this by at least identifying the information you need to find and copy, and they may be able to download that information automatically.

The Internet offers a wealth of information, and Internet search engines are effective in finding that information, especially if you know how they work and what you can do to improve your search results. Determining whether you found good, reputable information is another story. In chapter 9, we look at how to evaluate the information you found.

Vocabulary

advanced search	limiters
basic search	metasearch engines
domain	phrase searching
field searching	relevancy ranking
implied Boolean And	truncation

Questions

What limits can be applied to Internet searches?

How is a metasearch similar to a federated search?

What is relevancy ranking, and how does it work?

Which Internet search engine allows you to exclude terms from your search, and how do you do it?

How does truncation work in Internet search engines?

Assignment

Find two webpages with the .com domain, two webpages with the .edu domain, and two webpages with the .gov domain that you would consider using in your research on your topic. Record the search you used to find the items and the author, title, and URL of each item. See the example in Figure 6.1.

Search Statement for .Com webpages		
"global warming" whales population site:.com		
.COM WEBPAGES		
	AUTHOR	**TITLE**	**URL**
1.	Stefan Lovgren	Global Warming May Be Keeping Gray Whale Numbers Down	http://news.nationalgeographic.com/news/2007/09/070910-gray-whales.html
2.		Warming causing gray whales to lose weight, say scientists	http://www.breitbart.com/article.php?id=070712072227.r2enhwme&show_article=1
Search Statement for .Edu webpages		
"global warming" whales population site:.edu		
.EDU WEBPAGES		
1.	Alison Rieser	Whales, Whaling, and the Warming Oceans	http://lawdigitalcommons.bc.edu/cgi/viewcontent.cgi?-article=1013&context=ealr&sei-redir=1#search=%22%C3%A2%C2%80%C2%9Cglobal+warming%C3%A2%C2%80%C2%9D+whales+population+site:.edu%22
2.	Martin Taylor	Population Viability Analysis for the Southern Resident Population of the Killer Whale *(Orcinus orca)*	http://courses.washington.edu/mb351/readings/taylor_plater.pdf

Figure 6.1: Internet Search Worksheet.

Search Statement for .Gov webpages			
"global warming" whales population site:.gov			
.GOV WEBPAGES			
1.	Charles H Greene and Andrew J Pershing	Climate and the conservation biology of North Atlantic right whales: the right whale at the wrong time?	http://www.nmfs.noaa.gov/pr/sars/improvement/pdfs/climate_change_right_whales.pdf
2.		Northern Right Whale	http://www.maine.gov/ifw/wildlife/species/endangered_species/northern_right_whale/index.htm

Figure 6.1: (*Continued*)

CHAPTER 7

Librarians and Library Services

All the information you have read in the previous chapters can be difficult to remember. Fortunately, you do not have to remember it all. Libraries are not just places to access databases and check out a book. They are places that specialize in providing students with research assistance. In other words, they exist to help you find the information you need.

The Librarian

Librarians have very unique jobs. One of the most important aspects of their job is to provide research help. Librarians are professional question answerers. They are getting paid to answer questions. More to the point, they are getting paid to answer *your* questions. Librarians staff a reference desk, but the terminology can be confusing. Some libraries call it the help desk or question desk, but no matter what it is called, the reference desk is where you find the librarian who is currently assigned to help answer your questions.

If a librarian at the reference desk is not busy helping someone, then they are waiting for you to ask a question. You may feel intimidated or a little embarrassed to approach the librarian. They might look busy, frazzled, old, confused, or mean. It is normal to have reservations. In fact, there is a term for it: library anxiety. However, the more you know about libraries and the role of librarians, the less anxiety you will have (Gross and Latham 2007), and one of the best ways to learn what your library can do to help you is to ask the librarian. So if you are nervous, take a deep breath and approach the librarian. You should expect and receive courteous and professional service.

Research Help

Librarians will be able to help you with many facets of your research. They can help you pick a database to search. They can help you find good search terms. They can help you formulate your search statement, and they can show you what special features a database has and how to use them, like getting citations for the items on your marked list. They can help you search the catalog, find books on the shelf, and find a reference source. They can help you find out what journals the library has available in full text and in print.

Library Instruction

Besides the personalized help you can get from a librarian at the reference desk, librarians also teach groups of students how to use library resources. This is called library instruction or information literacy instruction. Your instructor may arrange to take your class to the library or have the librarian come to your class and show you some databases and search techniques tailored to your class. Library instruction is a good introduction to finding the information you need, but because of the limited time, it is broad in scope and cannot answer all of your questions. In fact, it might give you questions you did not know you had. That is good. That is part of the purpose of library instruction, to raise awareness and generate new questions. Be sure to ask these questions during the library instruction session or at the reference desk when you begin your research.

Interlibrary Loan

If you find an article that is not available in full text either in a database or in print, or if you know of a book you need but that the library does not own, then you can use interlibrary loan (ILL). This is an important service that libraries offer. Through interlibrary loan, libraries have access to more materials than they can afford to buy on their own. You will need to fill out a form, either print or electronic, in order to use ILL, but the service is often free for materials that are located within an affiliated group of libraries. Charges may apply to materials that come from outside this group or beyond a geographical area, such as the state you are in.

The most important caveat concerning ILL is that it takes time. Articles are commonly transmitted electronically from the lending library, the library that has the material, to the borrowing library, the library where you are located. Using this method, an electronic copy of the articles can arrive in one or two days. Books need to be physically shipped, and that means it could take a week or two for a book to show up. How fast an item arrives depends on a number of factors that are beyond the control of your local library. It is a good idea to start your research early not only so that you are not rushing to get it done at the last minute, but also so you can get all the information you need and take advantage of services like ILL, if necessary.

Librarians are your allies in the research process. They know how to find information and what resources and services the library has that can be of assistance to you. Their job is to help you find this information and use these resources and services efficiently and effectively. Be sure to take advantage of this service and ask your librarian for help.

Vocabulary

borrowing library

information literacy instruction

interlibrary loan

lending library

librarian

library anxiety

library instruction

reference desk

Questions

What is library instruction?

What is library anxiety, and how can it be overcome?

What kinds of help can you get from a librarian?

How can interlibrary loan help you with your research?

Assignment

Write three questions related to your research that you could ask a librarian. An example would be, "What is the best database to use to find information on global warming's impact on whales?"

CHAPTER 8

Evaluation and the Research Process

What Is Evaluation?

Evaluation for the purposes of this textbook has three parts. You evaluate your research process, you evaluate the information you find, and you evaluate your final product. *Evaluation* means examining your work or the work of others and making an informed judgment, not based on opinion or belief, but supported by facts, about the quality of that work.

Evaluation is based on critical thinking. Critical thinking is an active, intellectual process of logical thinking based on sound evidence. Critical thinking includes analyzing, comparing, contrasting, generalizing, investigating, experimenting, creating, conceptualizing, synthesizing, and evaluating information to achieve a goal, such as solving a problem, planning a course of action, or writing a research paper.

Critical thinkers should be able to admit a lack of understanding or information; ask pertinent questions; assess arguments; examine beliefs, assumptions, and opinions and weigh them against facts; suspend judgment until all facts have been gathered and considered; adjust opinions when new facts are found; understand the importance of context; reject information that is incorrect or irrelevant; recognize and correct discrepancies; explore and imagine alternatives; make connections between seemingly unrelated ideas; draw conclusions from a set of facts; submit their ideas and experiments for peer review; accept challenges and criticism to their work; listen carefully to others; and offer feedback and engage in reflective skepticism. These four sources were used to put together the proceeding definition of critical thinking and list of characteristics of critical thinkers: Foundation for Critical Thinking (1997), J. Lynn McBrien and Ronald Brandt (1997), Ken Petress (2004) and Thelma Riddell (2007).

Critical-thinking skills are vital to the evaluation process. The list is long, but it can be summed up as questioning yourself, your process, the information, and your results, then answering the questions you have posed and arriving at conclusions. It is using facts and solid reasoning to support the answers you find and give. You will use different sets of skills for each of the three parts of evaluation. It is important to remember that evaluation is a process. It is continual. You are always evaluating and using your critical-thinking skills.

Evaluating Your Research Process

We have already talked about evaluating the research process, but we have not called it evaluation. When we talked about modifying your search to find more or fewer articles, we were talking about evaluating your search.

You cannot evaluate your research process until you try a search in a database, and at that point, you have already made decisions about the database, search statement, and keywords. If your search succeeded in finding a sufficient number of relevant articles, then you are not going to need to evaluate your research process. But if your search failed, where do you begin? Do you start with your database selection, your search statement or something else? Any of these in any combination could be the problem, and that is what makes evaluating your research process difficult. There is not a set order in which to do the evaluation, instead, as you evaluate each of these areas, you need to keep the others in mind and know how a change to one could impact the others. Here are the parts of the research process to evaluate:

- The search statement
- The keywords
- The database selection
- The research question.

Search Statement

The search statement is one of the easiest parts of the research process to evaluate. The search statement is your use of the Boolean operators, the phrase operator, truncation, and the other mechanics of the search. You should be using the database's advanced search screen, which resembles the Database Search Worksheet from chapter 5, because it is a good visual representation of your search. You can make changes to your search statement and see how those changes impact your search.

If your search statement finds too many records, then the database is not the problem. Your search statement may have too few items that are being Anded together, or you misused the Or operator, which broadened your search in an unexpected way. If you used an Or statement in your search, make sure that Or is being used to group together synonyms and that the group of synonyms is being Anded to another keyword or concept.

Keywords

Keywords have a great impact on your search results. The keyword "fracking," a term used for the process of pumping fluids into a well to increase the recovery of oil and gas, returns only a handful of scholarly articles from a general database. However, the phrase "hydraulic fracturing," the technical term for "fracking," returns hundreds of scholarly articles in that same database. With such a small set of articles returned for the keyword "fracking," it is nearly impossible to combine that term with any other and find any results. For example, "fracking and earthquakes" found 0 scholarly articles, whereas "hydraulic fracturing and earthquakes" found 12.

Choosing the right keywords to search is the difference between a successful search and a failed one. Finding the right keywords can involve some trial and error and a little digging. Run your search statement in a database. Examine your results list to see if you find any articles that relate to your topic. Examine the item records for those articles and look for where your keywords show up in the record. Is it in the title or the abstract? Pay close attention to the subject terms used by the database to describe the article. Did one or more of your keywords show up here? If not, what terms were used? Do these terms describe your topic? If so, use these terms when you modify your search. That is how you will move from "fracking" to "hydraulic fracturing."

Database Selection

Which database you choose to search will have a big impact on your search results. You would not search for Shakespeare in BioOne, a database that covers biological science, but you *would* search for Shakespeare in MLA Bibliographies, which covers literature.

As we mentioned before, you can always start your search in a general database like Academic Search Premier, which covers all subject areas. Because it is a general database, it has breadth but not as much depth as a subject specific database. You will find a lot of information about Shakespeare or poison dart frogs in a general database, but you will find more in MLA Bibliographies and BioOne, respectively. More information may be confusing. However, more records for a keyword like Shakespeare or a phrase like "poison dart frogs" means that when you combine those terms with other ideas, you will be more likely to find the information you wanted. For example, this search

- shakespeare and authorship and "de vere"

found 4 scholarly articles in a general database. That same search in MLA Bibliographies found 19. This search

- "poison dart frog*" and pollution

found zero articles in our general database, but three were found in BioOne. Depending on your topic, your best choice may be a subject-specific database.

If you checked your search statement and it looks good, and if you tried your keywords and they seem appropriate, but still your search is not finding enough information, then the problem has to be the database you are searching. Move from a general to a subject-specific database. Switch from one subject-specific database to another, or if your library has federated searching, use that resource to find your articles and the databases that have them.

Research Question

If you tried changing your search statement, changing your keywords, and changing databases but still are not finding enough information, then you may have to take a step back and look at your research question. Is it too specific, too complicated, or too new? If your research question is based on a discovery made a month earlier, then it may be too new to have much written about it.

Try restating your research question. This could help you find other words to search or lead to a different search statement. It may help you think about different ways to approach your topic or different aspects of your topic that you may want to examine. This will help you change your keywords and your search statement. Make sure you are not searching for long phrases as these narrow your results greatly. Try searching each of your keywords individually to see if any of them are the problem. Finally, if nothing seems to be working, change your topic! Sometimes this is the best route to take. Your topic may simply be too obscure or too new to have much information. Additionally, remember that the librarian is there to help you with all aspects of your research process.

Vocabulary

critical thinking

database selection

evaluation

information

informed judgment

keywords

questioning

research process

research question

search statement

Questions

What is evaluation, and why is it important?

When evaluating your research process, what should you examine?

How do you determine if there is a problem with your search statement or keywords?

How does your choice of database impact your research process?

How can you fix a bad research question?

Assignment

Search a general database for a topic, and find articles from scholarly publications. Make note of what you find. Use synonyms for your keywords and search again. Compare and contrast your results. Which search retrieved more items and why? Pick a subject database and run both searches again. Which database returned more items and why? Where did your keywords show up in the records: title, subject, or another field?

For example, your searches could be

- "global warming" and cities and "sea level"
- "climate change" and refugees

Both of these searches are trying to capture the idea of how global warming's impact on ocean levels will affect human life in coastal cities.

CHAPTER 9

Evaluating Information

When you find information, you need to evaluate it. It does not matter where you found the information, it needs to be evaluated. You do not want to use something that is outdated, uninformed, or factually incorrect. This not only impacts the development of your understanding of the topic, but it hurts the quality of your research project, which in turn leads to a lower grade than expected.

To ensure that you are using only good, quality information, you need to evaluate its relevance, purpose, and validity.

Relevance

The first step is to examine your information for relevance. You can find a lot of information quickly, but not all of it is going to be relevant to your research. If the information is not on topic or does not relate to your research, then cut it from your pool of information. You may learn something interesting or important from the remaining information you found, but you need to ask if you are likely to quote or summarize it in your research? If the answer is yes or maybe, then keep it. Otherwise, it is just another piece of information that did not make the cut. Relevance is that easy. Purpose and validity require more effort and may eliminate a number of your relevant articles from your pool of information.

Purpose

Purpose is the "why" of the information. Why was this information created? What is the purpose of presenting the information in this way?

Was the information designed to inform, entertain, editorialize, or persuade? Was it intended to provide background information or to delve deep into a topic? Purpose includes the scope and depth of the information and the style used to present the information.

Scope and Depth

Scope is what is covered, how it is covered, and what is not covered in an information source. We have talked about scope before. We mentioned broad and narrow scopes. A broad scope can provide an overview, while a narrow scope may examine only one very specific aspect of a topic. *Depth* is how much detail there is in the coverage of the information. Information has depth when it spends time on the details.

For example, a reference source has a 2-page article on George Washington's leadership during the Revolutionary War. A magazine has a 6-page article on the same topic. A journal has an 18-page article, and a book has 300 pages on the topic. The scope is the same, but the depth is very different. Conversely, a journal article may give you Washington's strategy and maneuvers for one battle in 18 pages, while the 300-page book gives you that same information, plus that same level of detail, for a number of other battles that Washington fought. In this case, the information sources have the same depth, but different scopes.

Knowing the scope and depth of the information you found will tell you what kind of information you can expect and whether the information is designed to give you an overview of a broad topic, or illuminate the finest details of a very narrow topic, or something in-between. It may also help you realize what is missing from the information, what cannot be included because of its scope and depth, or what should be included but is not. It should also give you an idea on how to use the information in your research, whether for background or to support a point in your hypothesis, to help you see the big picture, or to help you come to a specific conclusion.

Style

Style is how the information is conveyed. It includes the words the author chooses to use and the intent or purpose of those words. Most of the information sources you will encounter while doing research will be designed primarily to inform, to impart information and facts about events and research projects. Besides informing, information sources may be designed to entertain, editorialize, or persuade. A summer action film, a television sitcom, and a song are intended to entertain. They may include a life-lesson designed to inform, but that is not their primary purpose.

A newspaper is designed to inform, but it also includes an editorial page where staff writers and readers can editorialize. Editorializing is a way to express opinions. Opinions are not facts and may or may not be supported by facts. An economist editorializing about a banking crisis may have an informed opinion. She may know more about the crisis than the average person, but it is still an opinion, and facts may not bear it out.

Politicians often present information in a manner designed to persuade people to vote for them. As an example, let us presume there is a politician who believes he can get elected by running on an anti-egg consumption platform. He states that Americans eat 247 eggs per person per year, and that is too much. He continues by saying that there is a whole segment of the population that is harmed by the cholesterol in eating so many eggs and that egg consumption increases fat intake, which is bad for your health. If you vote for him, he concludes, he will reduce egg consumption and increase the health of Americans. His speech is persuasive, but where did his information come from, and is it valid?

Our politician's statements have one fact and two misuses of information. According to *Statistical Abstract* (Per Capita Consumption of Major Food Commodities: 1980–2008 2011), in 2008, the most recent year that information is available, we did consume 247 eggs each. That is the only thing our politician got right. He used an article by Ruxton (2010) to take information out of context and misuse it. That article states that the cholesterol from eggs is bad for people with familial hypercholesterolaemia (2010, 50), a condition that occurs in 1 out of every 500 people (Familial Hypercholesterolemia 2011), our politicians "whole segment of the population." The article also states that egg consumers who eat their eggs with more than 50 grams of bacon or sausages had higher daily intakes of fat than those who did not (Ruxton 2010, 49). The article does not state that eating eggs leads to a fatty, unhealthy diet as our politician implies. In fact, the article is about how eggs are a good thing to include in our diets. This is the exact opposite of what our politician wants us to believe. Will his persuasive use of language earn him support, or will people see through his misuse of information, broad generalizations, unsupported claims, and distortion of the facts?

This is a good introduction to our next section on validity, where you will examine the information that is presented as opposed to how it is presented.

Validity

Validity is quality analysis. It asks how good the information is and bases the answer on a critical analysis of all aspects of the information, including its timeliness, accuracy, and authority.

Timeliness

Timeliness is the age of the information. It includes not only when the information was created or published, but also how old the sources of information were that were used in creating the information you are evaluating. If an article was published 10 years ago, is it old or bad information? The answer is, that depends. An article that age in the medical field may be horribly outdated and even dangerously incorrect. An article the same age in the humanities might reflect the best current thinking. A news source about Hurricane Katrina from that time period may be old, but it may be the best source to get firsthand accounts and an understanding of the impact of the events as they unfolded in the hurricane's aftermath. You need to look beyond a simple measure of the age of the document and examine its field and the purpose you would use the information for to determine its value.

Check the ages of the references used in information sources. For example, a scholarly article could have been published yesterday, making its timeliness look very appealing. However, when you look at the publication dates of the references cited at the end of the article, you find that there is nothing newer than 10 years old. What does that mean for the information presented in the article? Is it up to date? No matter the field, shouldn't there be something newer? What if all the citations were from the last year? Certainly that means the information is up to date, but what if the article was about the history and development of an idea? Shouldn't there be some older sources? Would a range of dates that includes older and newer material indicate more thorough research? Maybe. What if all the sources cited were from the same author or the same journal? Would that be a bad thing? Probably. Are the cited journals and authors reputable? You will have to analyze this information on an article-by-article basis.

Accuracy

You will need to bring all of your critical-thinking skills to bear when you evaluate your information for accuracy. For example, you are reading on article on Mars that states that the average daytime temperature is a very pleasant 75° F. You make a quick check of *The New Encyclopædia Britannica* and find the mean surface temperature is –82° F (Mars 2010, 873). Your fact checking has found a significant discrepancy. You check other sources, including *The World Almanac and Book of Facts, 2011* (Janssen 2010, 347) and *Encyclopedia of Astronomy and Astrophysics* (Moroz 2001, 1669). You find that they all agree with the *Britannica*. The agreement of multiple, good sources indicate the accuracy of the information. Clearly, the article is not accurate. If there is no source cited for the incorrect temperature data, then the author is uninformed or trying to deceive. If the author cited a source for the incorrect temperature data, then the author either did not bother to check his sources, or worse, he did check and does not care that the information is wrong.

The number and quality of the sources cited by an author has an impact on its accuracy. An article with 50 citations from good sources is probably more accurate than an article with 1 citation. An article with citations from 50 different good sources is probably more accurate than an article with 50 citations to the same source. The quantity of citations an article has in itself is not a measure of accuracy. More does not necessarily mean better. It does indicate some level of thought, research, and fact checking that went into the article's writing.

What if an author of an article includes 50 citations, but half of them are to other articles that she wrote? Self-citation is a common practice. However, while a few citations to an author's own work are fine, multiple citations are not. Can you think of why? If you cite yourself too much, it weakens your authority, and at some point, it becomes your opinion.

Finally, arguments put forward by the authors should be logical and supported by facts. You should be able to follow the authors' logic from hypothesis to arguments to conclusion. Their reasoning should not be unnecessarily complicated. It should flow from the facts and build upon them. There should be no gaps in their thinking, no leaps of logic. The conclusion should be constructed from all the reasoning that came before, and the whole construct should feel solid. All of this should be supported by facts, not opinions, and these facts should be cited, so they can be checked.

If you are reading an article that talks about aspects of Romeo's character from Shakespeare's *Romeo and Juliet*, how do you check the facts? This is not a scientific article. No experiment was conducted.

No study of animal populations was undertaken. There are no tables of figures or charts presented. How can something like this be supported by facts? The facts in this case come from the text. If the article you are reading states that Romeo speaks with a French accent, is very tall, and has a long, red beard, then you should be able to find mentions of all three of these statements in the text of the play, and they should be cited by the author of the article.

Authority

Authority is the people responsible for the information. In most cases, these people are the publishers and the authors. The publishers bring to the table their reputation. It can be hard to determine publishers' reputations. However, Oxford University Press would have a better reputation than Southwest County Community College and Pet Boarding Press. The *Harvard Business Review* would have a better reputation than Uncle Bob's Business Review. While brand name recognition is something that has to be built, you can check the types of materials that a publisher produces, for example, books, journals, DVDs, and so forth. Do they specialize in specific subjects or formats? How much do they publish? While bigger may not always be better, it is an indication of success. How well reviewed are the materials they publish? Have their authors published other books or journal articles? What are the authors' credentials?

Journals have reputations as well, and like other publishers and producers of information, there are brand names that have a reputation for quality. You can use the same methodology to check on a journal. Look at the types of articles they publish, check their authors' credentials and publications, and fact check some of their articles.

Book, magazine, and news publishers have editors who should be doing some quality checking. This is no guarantee of quality, especially if the publisher is not interested in facts but instead is interested in promoting a point of view. Journals have the peer review process. A peer review involves the editors of the journal sending blind submissions that are being considered for publication to peers. A blind submission is an article without any author information. This is withheld to prevent any possible favoritism. Peers are scholars in the field. The peers evaluate the articles independently from each other and determine if the articles are good enough to be published in their journal. If there is agreement among the peers that an article should be published, then it will be published; otherwise, it will be rejected. The peer review process ensures a higher level of quality.

The authors are the other part of the authority equation. An author should provide his or her credentials. In other words, an author should tell you his degree, what it is in, perhaps where he got it, and where he is currently employed. For example, if we look back to our article on Romeo, if the author has a PhD in English literature from Yale University and currently teaches Shakespeare studies at the University of Wisconsin, she has more authority than if she has a BA degree in English literature from Fly by Night University where she also teaches. What if our PhD from Yale wrote an article about the effects of incarceration on juveniles? She would not have much authority because she is working outside of her field.

You should check an author to see what else he or she has published. Databases make this easy. When you have found an article that you are considering, you can click on the authors' names to search for other articles they have written that are indexed in that particular database. How many more articles have they written? What journals did they appear in? Are the sources they cited good? Once again, more is not necessarily an indication of quality, but it does indicate a track record. Some databases show how many times an article has been cited by other sources. This is also a valuable piece of information. If the article has been cited many times by other authors, it has had an impact. What if the article you found that best supports your hypothesis is the only article written by that author, and it has not been cited by other authors? Should you use it? The answer is yes, if the other elements of timeliness, accuracy, and authority are all good.

As a matter of course, authors should provide contact information, such as their email address. This courtesy allows to you ask a question about their research or clarify a point that you did not understand. Authors should be willing to talk about their work and exchange ideas.

It is important to evaluate the information you find to ensure that you have good quality information that supports your research and answers your information need. Evaluating information is a skill. The more you do it, the better at it you become, and the easier it is to weed out the bad while keeping the good. Good information makes for good arguments, good papers, and, ultimately, good grades, while bad information will drag you down. Good information also makes for good decisions. So be sure to cast a critical eye on the information you find.

Vocabulary

accuracy

agreement

authority

citation

credentials

degree

depth

editor

editorialize

entertain

fact checking

inform

peer

peer review

persuade

purpose

relevance

reputation

scope

self-citation

style

timeliness

validity

Questions

What is the purpose of evaluating information?

What is the peer review process, and why is it important?

How does style impact the purpose of information?

Which of the three evaluation criteria is the most important and why?

How is timeliness impacted by the discipline or the type of information source?

What effects do an author's credentials have on the validity of the information presented?

Assignment

Use the information you found for the assignment in chapter 5. Compare and contrast the information you found from the different information types. How would you use the information from each source?

Pick one of your journal articles and evaluate the information for relevance, purpose, and validity. Be specific. How does the journal article meet or not meet the criteria? What qualities does the article have that would make you want to use it or not want to use it in your research? End by assigning a grade to the article. See the example in Figure 9.1.

TOPIC		
The effects of climate change on whale populations		

JOURNAL ARTICLE		
AUTHOR	**TITLE**	**SOURCE**
Whitehead, Hal; McGill, Brian; Worm, Boris	Diversity of deep-water cetaceans in relation to temperature: implications for ocean warming	Ecology Letters, Nov2008, Vol. 11 Issue 11, p1198-1207

RELEVANCE
This article is very relevant to my topic. It covers what I am researching.

PURPOSE
Scope: The scope of the article is broad as it uses sights of many different marine mammals over the course of many years as its dataset to show the movements of
Depth: The article's focus is narrow. It is about the relocation of marine mammals in relation to rising ocean temperatures. The article has a lot of information about this topic. So it has depth.

VALIDITY
Timeliness: The article was published in 2008, and it has data from 2007, which is very good. It is one of the most current articles relevant to my topic, and the information is still of great value.
Accuracy: The article used observational studies taken over the course of many years for its data. There is an explanation of the mathematical models used to analyze the data, and charts and tables are given. This should be accurate. There is also a bibliography with many citations to other scholarly sources, including both current sources and older sources. This indicates a high level of research and should mean accurate information.

Figure 9.1: Information Evaluation Worksheet.

Authority:
Ecology Letters is published by Wiley-Blackwell, a very large and reputable publishing company that publishes scholarly books and journals in all subject areas. The article was peer reviewed and selected for publication. The authors work in the department of biology at Dalhousie University in Canada, and contact information is provided. So the authors have the appropriate knowledge of the subject. The lead author, Hal Whitehead, has many other articles indexed in Academic Search Premier that deal with whales, so he has authority.
GRADE
A

Figure 9.1: (*Continued*)

CHAPTER 10

Evaluating Your Product

The last piece of the evaluation puzzle is to evaluate your product. Because we are focused on the research process and the paper that results from that process, our evaluation of the product will be limited to evaluating your research paper. Remember that evaluation is a process. It is continuous. You should not just evaluate your product when it is finished, but as you are working on it. You do not want to write a term paper, then decide it is bad and have to start over from scratch. With that in mind, we will start by looking at organizing your paper.

Organization

After you have gathered and read your research, and before you start writing your paper, writing an outline will help you organize your thoughts. An outline lays out the path you are going to follow from hypothesis through arguments to the conclusion. With an outline in place, you can organize your research and plan when you will mention which articles and ideas. You want your paper to have a logical flow to it.

Evaluate your outline before your start writing. Does it cover all the points you want to make? Are they in a logical order? You should also evaluate your outline as you work on your paper. Is the information still in a logical order? Is there something you forgot or that just occurred to you that you want to add? If so, move sections around if necessary and adjust your outline. Are you going off on tangents and losing the focus of your paper? If so, then remove those sections and adjust your outline.

Logic

You should evaluate your logic, your reasoning, as you write your paper. Your logic should be straight forward, easy to understand, and stated in a clear, direct manner. The arguments you use to support your reasoning should, in turn, be supported by the facts and information you found in your research. This gives validity to your arguments.

When evaluating your logic, start by asking if your argument make sense. Does it build on what came before it in a logical manner? Does it help lay the groundwork for your next argument? How is this argument supported by your research? Which facts from which articles and other sources support this argument? Even when you state original thoughts of your own, they should be subject to the same evaluation and supported by evidence from your research.

Your conclusion is your final statement. It links to your thesis statement at the very beginning of your paper, which you should now state that you have proved or disproved. It is the culmination of all the evidence you presented along the way, and like all your previous arguments, it should hold up to the scrutiny of an evaluation.

Proofreading

Before you print or send your paper to your instructor, you need to proofread it. Proofreading is the final step in evaluating your paper, and while it can be done during the writing process, proofreading needs to be done after you finish your paper as well. When you proofread, you are looking for minor errors in your spelling and grammar. You have already looked for and corrected errors in your organization and logic.

Word processors conveniently mark spelling and grammar errors for you to review, but the little red and blue lines that highlight mistakes are easy to miss and ignore. That means you need to look carefully for them. Spell checkers are great, but they cannot tell you if you used the wrong word, and they will struggle with many proper names. Grammar checkers are helpful, but the English language is very complicated and nuances can be missed. In the following sentence, the letter "r" was left out of "horses":

■ "Wild hoses roam the Nevada high country."

The spell checker found no misspelled words. The grammar checker recognized a grammatically correct sentence with the appropriate agreement between the noun and verb. However, your instructor will see a sentence that does not make sense, and you may get marked down for this simple mistake.

Do not rely on your spell checker and grammar checker to catch all of your mistakes. Be sure to proofread your paper and look for errors or have a friend proofread your paper while you proofread hers. This is your last chance to evaluate your paper and make changes before turning it in. An organized, well-reasoned paper that is free of spelling and grammatical errors will impress your instructors.

Vocabulary

arguments

conclusion

evidence

grammar checker

logic

organization

outline

proofreading

reasoning

spell checker

Questions

Why is evaluating your product or paper important?

What impact does an outline have on a research paper?

How can unsupported arguments affect a research paper?

What should good reasoning look like?

How do spelling errors impact the impression made by a paper?

Assignment

Write an outline for a research paper on your topic. Your outline should have at least three sections aside from the introduction and conclusion. Then write a comment about why you think this is a good outline.

Next, write one of the arguments that you would use in this paper. It should be supported by a journal article that you found earlier. Then write a comment that explains why this is a good argument and how it is supported by your research. Include the citation information, the author, title, and source information, for the article you use. See the example in Figure 10.1.

OUTLINE
I.   Introduction: Climate change has had a negative impact on whales. II. Climate change and oceans III. Climate change and whale habitats IV. Climate change and whale populations V. Conclusion

COMMENT
The outline moves from a general overview of climate change and its impact on oceans to the specific impacts it has had on whales. This should give the paper a logical flow.

ARGUMENT
Climate change has raised ocean temperatures, and this has led to a change in range where certain whale species are found.

COMMENT
This argument comes directly from the research in the article below, which shows how rising ocean temperatures have impacted the range of a number of whale species. It is clear, and shows a direct link between climate change and whale habitats.

JOURNAL ARTICLE		
AUTHOR	**TITLE**	**SOURCE**
Whitehead, Hal; McGill, Brian; Worm, Boris	Diversity of deep-water cetaceans in relation to temperature: implications for ocean warming	*Ecology Letters,* Nov 2008, Vol. 11 Issue 11, p. 1198–1207

Figure 10.1: Paper Evaluation Worksheet.

CHAPTER 11

Using Information

In the previous three chapters, we looked at evaluation. The decision was made to keep all of the chapters on evaluation together to cover all of the aspects of this topic at the same time. However, evaluation of your product, which is your research paper, would occur after the application of information. Using information means that you have gathered information, analyzed it, and now are going to use it to answer a question, solve a problem, or write a research paper that proves your hypothesis.

Communicating Information

One of the first decisions you need to make after doing your research is to decide how you will present your results. It is not enough just to research an information need. You need to communicate the results of that research to others. As a student, this often means writing a research paper or participating in a group project. When you start your career, it could mean a report to your colleagues or clients. It could mean a PowerPoint presentation at a conference, an article published in a scholarly journal, or a conversation with a friend.

The medium used to communicate the information you find may be specified by your instructor, or it may be left up to you. If you get to choose the medium, then be sure to pick one that is conducive to the information you want to present. For example, if you interview veterans about their experiences, then a video or audio recording may work very well. If you want to document an event, then photographs or a video recording may be your best option. Perhaps combining your photos with a written report or creating a website to showcase your videos would work well. You may have a lot of data that you need to present in tables or charts, and this information may work well with a written paper or a presentation where you can explain your charts. In any event, you have many options for communicating the information you found. Be sure to take a minute to think about the most effective method of presenting your information.

Using Information

Using information to answer your information need is bigger than doing homework for a class. You will need to use information to solve problems and answer questions throughout your life. It could help you develop a marketing campaign based on the information you gathered about the characteristics of the consumers you are targeting for your product. It could help you find a good, used car for the money you have to spend or determine which presidential candidate is telling more of the truth. No matter what the need, you should apply the good information you found to answer that need or that question and do so in an ethical manner.

The ethical use of information is one of the most important concepts in information literacy. It is the third and final part of our definition of information literacy, which includes finding and evaluating information. Using information ethically means using information legally and giving credit to others for their ideas.

Intellectual Property, Copyright, and Fair Use

Intellectual property is the product of your research, hard work, and imagination. Intellectual property is "creations of the mind" (World Intellectual Property Organization 2011). Legally, your intellectual property could lead to a patent, trademark, or copyright, which would grant you, as the owner, certain rights (Intellectual Property 2011). Information literacy is primarily concerned with the use of copyrighted materials because you will use copyrighted materials in your research and in your daily life.

Copyright is a legal form of protection provided to "the authors of 'original works of authorship,' including literary, dramatic, musical, artistic and certain other intellectual works" (U. S. Copyright Office 2008, 1). These rights include authorizing people to display, perform, or copy your work or create derivative works, such as turning your novel into a movie.

You do not have to apply for copyright. It is automatic. If you create a webpage, it is copyrighted from the moment it is "fixed in a copy," which is an "object from which a work can be read" (U. S. Copyright Office 2008, 3). Copyright is very easily obtained, and the rights it gives the creator are substantial, but there are some situations where the creator's rights are limited. One of these limits is *terms of use*. For example, you may sign up for an account on a website that allows you to create posts in response to articles published there. In order to create your account, you have to agree to the terms of use, which may state that the website has the right to distribute, copy, and create derivative works from your posts. In other words, you have given up your copyright. You own the copyright to your term papers and whatever else you create, unless you signed a statement giving up those rights.

Another very important limit to a creator's copyright protection is called *fair use*. Fair use grants everyone limited rights to use copyrighted works. This includes using copyrighted works for the purpose of scholarship or research (U. S. Copyright Office 2009). There are also four factors listed in the law to consider when determining if your use of copyrighted materials is fair. The first is how you plan to use the material. Will it be used for commercial gain, or is it for nonprofit, educational use? Next is the nature of the document you plan to use. If the document is largely factual, it favors fair use because facts and ideas cannot be copyrighted, but "the particular way authors have expressed themselves" can (U. S. Copyright Office 2009). The third factor is the amount of the work you intend to use. The more you use, the less fair that use is. The fourth factor is how your use of the copyrighted work impacts its market value. For example, if you make a copy of a song and distribute it to 100 of your friends, you have denied the artist, the copyright holder, 100 potentials sales and the royalties from those sales. You have violated copyright, broken the law, and you are legally accountable for your actions. If you are not sure if the use you plan for a copyrighted work is legal under the fair use doctrine, then you can always contact the copyright holder and ask permission for that use.

Many works are in the public domain. Works that are in the public domain are not protected by copyright and are free to be used as you see fit. This includes everything published before 1923 (Fishman 2008, 5). Authors may place their works in the public domain or use the Creative Commons License, which allows you to copy, distribute, and perform the work (Text of Creative Commons Attribution 2011). Government documents are not covered by copyright law and are therefore in the public domain. However, items in the public domain or available under the Creative Commons license still need to be quoted accurately and cited appropriately, or you will have plagiarized.

Plagiarism

Plagiarism is claiming someone else's ideas as your own. It is a lie told to the audience by your work, and it is theft from the true creator of the idea. If you forget to cite a source in your research paper, you have committed plagiarism even though that was not your intent. Plagiarism, intended or accidental, has consequences. The consequences vary by severity of the infraction and your school's policies. You may receive a light punishment, like receiving a failing grade on the assignment, or your punishment might be more severe. You may receive a failing grade for the class, be placed on academic probation, or even dismissed from school. There are real-world consequences for plagiarism, as well. Recently, the German Defense Minister, Karl-Theodor zu Guttenberg, was forced to resign his cabinet position when it was learned that he had plagiarized information on his thesis (Dempsey 2011).

In the past, your instructors relied on their experience and knowledge of your previous work to detect plagiarism. Now they can use services like Turnitin (http://turnitin.com/static/index.php), which make it easier for them to detect plagiarism. Turnitin is a very large service that compares your electronic document to all the other papers turned in from your class, all the other documents from all the other classes that use Turnitin from across the country, and to sites across the Web to find matches to the wording in your document. Your instructor checks the matches in your paper to make sure that your information sources are cited. If you plagiarized your information or turned in somebody else's paper, then consequences will follow.

Quoting, Paraphrasing, and Summarizing Information

The simplest way to avoid plagiarism is to attribute the information you use from the sources you found. This means quoting, paraphrasing, or summarizing the information from the sources you use in your paper and then properly citing those sources.

Using information from other sources is a great way to support your arguments and to help prove your hypotheses. Include quotes in your paper when the exact wording from the source is important to your argument. You may also choose to paraphrase from your information sources. Paraphrasing is restating the author's point in your own words, perhaps to shorten the passage from the original. This can be difficult to do. You cannot use the original author's phrasing. If you find that you cannot restate without using phrases from the original work, then you are better off using a quotation.

You may also choose to summarize an information source in your paper. A summary is a short overview of the work written in your own words and covering the main ideas of the work. Summarizing is different than paraphrasing. Paraphrasing should represent an idea or passage from the work and not the whole work like a summary.

Whether you quote, paraphrase, or summarize in your paper the information you found, it should be in service to your thoughts and ideas on the topic. The information you found and use in your paper should provide the evidence that supports *your* conclusions. They should not make up your whole paper.

Citing Your Information

After quoting, paraphrasing, or summarizing an information source in your paper, you need to attribute that information to its source. You do this with a citation. A citation has two parts. The first is the in-text citation, which gives very brief information, such as the author's last name and year of publication, or it may simply be a number. This is then associated with an alphabetical bibliography or numbered notes, which is the second part of the citation and includes the full bibliographic information. What constitutes the full bibliographic information depends on the type of information source you are citing and the citation style you are using. It includes, but is not limited to, the names of the authors, title of the piece, and publication information.

There are literally thousands of different citation styles that are specific to different disciplines and journals. The APA style, developed by the American Psychological Association, is used in psychology. The MLA style, from the Modern Language Association, is used in English and humanities classes. Your instructor should assign a citation style for you to use. This style will determine how both your in-text citation and bibliography should look. Figures 11.1 and 11.2 show a book and a journal article in each of the formats mentioned here. You will need to look closely to see the minor differences between them.

There are many ways to get help with citing sources. There are books from the creators of the format, such as the *MLA Handbook* and

STYLE	IN-TEXT CITATION	BIBLIOGRAPHY
APA	(Hough, 2010, p. 21)	Hough, S. (2010). *Predicting the unpredictable: The tumultuous science of earthquake prediction.* Princeton, NJ: Princeton University Press.
MLA	(Hough 21)	Hough, Susan. *Predicting the Unpredictable: The Tumultuous Science of Earthquake Prediction.* Princeton: Princeton UP, 2010. Print.

Figure 11.1: Book Citation in Two Formats.

STYLE	IN-TEXT CITATION	BIBLIOGRAPHY
APA	(Bormann, 2011, p. 329)	Bormann, P. (2011). From earthquake prediction research to time-variable seismic hazard assessment applications. *Pure & Applied Geophysics, 168*(1/2), 329–366. doi:10.1007/s00024-010-0114-0
MLA	(Bormann 329)	Bormann, Peter. "From Earthquake Prediction Research to Time-Variable Seismic Hazard Assessment Applications." *Pure & Applied Geophysics* 168.1/2 (2011): 329–366.

Figure 11.2: Journal Citation in Two Formats.

the *Publication Manual* for MLA and APA, respectively. Then there are books like *A Pocket Style Manual* that cover three major formats in one short book. All of these books can be found in your library's reference collection. Websites such as *Research and Documentation Online* (http://bcs.bedfordstmartins.com/resdoc5e) cover the major formats and make it easy to find specific examples for your specific needs. Any of these resources will help you with many examples of how to cite books, journals, DVDs, and other media in all their possible permutations in the major formats.

Most commercial databases will generate a bibliographic citation in a few of the major formats. Websites such as Son of Citation Machine (http://citationmachine.net) and EasyBib will help you produce good citations and even have some shortcuts for finding books and other materials. Word processors have built-in features to help you create both your in-text citations and your bibliography, but you need to input all of your citation information.

Commercial software like EndNote and RefWorks (http://www.
refworks.com), along with freeware programs like Zotero, belong to a
class of programs called citation managers, which not only help you
generate your entire bibliography but help you track and organize all
of your research projects. They also have the benefit of "cite while
you write" add-ins for word processing programs such as Word and
Writer that make it easy to properly insert your in-text citation, then
generate your bibliography from all of the in-text cites you used. Additionally, these programs can import the full bibliographic information from many databases, so you do not have to do any typing of the
bibliographic information. These tools are time savers and very useful.
However, they also frequently make mistakes with your citations. For
example, if you import an article with its title in all capital letters into
one of these programs, your citation will have all capital letters, which
is not correct. It is important that you know what citations should
look like for the format you need to use in order to avoid these kinds
of mistakes. Be sure to consult official publications or style guides in
print or on the Web to make sure you understand how a citation should
appear.

Learning from the Experience

Finally, we want you to learn from the experience of finding information, writing papers, and citing sources. Ask yourself what you
would do differently next time? How would you improve your research process? How would you improve the quality of the sources
you found? How would you improve your paper? Answers to these
questions may be to use a citation manager to keep track of your research, to ask for help finding sources earlier in the process, to evaluate
sources more critically, to write an outline to help organize your paper,
or to double check the format of all citations.

While we want you to learn how to do these things better and more
efficiently, there is something much bigger than this about the learning process. At the beginning of this book, we talked about how we
are creatures of information. We are made from information. We create information, and we consume information. If we choose to, our
minds can always be open to new information, and we can always
be learning. When we learn something from the information we have
gathered, it becomes part of who we are. It helps us grow and become better human beings. Information we consume and synthesize
becomes knowledge. Knowledge changes who we are and who we
want to become. Using the knowledge we have gained can change the
world.

Vocabulary

bibliography	in-text citation
citation	medium
citation managers	notes
citation styles	paraphrasing
communicating information	plagiarism
copyright	public domain
ethical use of information	quoting
fair use	summarizing
intellectual property	using information

Questions

What does it mean to use information ethically?

What is fair use?

Is plagiarism illegal, and what are the consequences of plagiarizing?

How do you communicate the information you found?

What is a citation, and how do citation styles change the format of the citation?

Assignment

Write a research question, then find five sources, one from each of the following types of material: reference sources, books, magazines, journals, and the Internet. Choose a citation style, and write the in-text citation and the bibliographic entry for each of the items you found in the style you chose. Be sure to format the entries exactly as their style requires. See the example in Figure 11.3.

Research question	
What are the dangers of teenage drinking?	
Citation Style	
MLA	
Reference Source	(Hellmuth, Stuart, and Follansbee)
Book	(MacLachlan and Smyth 51)

Figure 11.3: Citation Worksheet.

News Source	(Hambleton E1)
Magazine	(Schwartz)
Journal	(Tapert, Calwell, and Burke 205)
Web site	(Center for Disease Control and Prevention)

Bibliography

Works Cited

Center for Disease Control and Prevention. "Fact Sheets: Underage Drinking."
    Center for Disease Control and Prevention. CDC, 20 July 2010. Web. 5 Aug
    2011.

Hambleton, Laura. "Bingeing Takes Toll on Teen Brains." *The Washington Post* 7
    Dec. 2010: E1. Print.

Hellmuth, Julianne C., Gregory L. Stuart, and Katherine W. Follansbee. "Underage
    Drinking." *Encyclopedia of Substance Abuse Prevention, Treatment, & Re-
    covery*. SAGE Reference Online, 2008. Web. 5 Aug. 2011.

MacLachlan, Malcolm, and Caroline Smyth, eds. *Binge Drinking and Youth Culture:
    Alternative Perspectives*. Dublin: Liffey Press, 2004. Print.

Schwartz, Emma. "A Host of Trouble." *U.S. News & World Report* 8 Oct. 2007: 47-
    50. *Academic Search Premier*. Web. 30 June 2011.

Tapert, Susan E., Lisa Calwell, and Christina Burke. "Alcohol and the Adolescent
    Brain: Human Studies." *Alcohol Research & Health* 28.4 (2004): 205–212.
    Print.

Figure 11.3: (*Continued*)

Works Cited

Accreditation. 2011. *Association of College and Research Libraries*. http://
www.ala.org/ala/mgrps/divs/acrl/issues/infolit/standards/accred/
accreditation.cfm.

American Association of School Librarians. 2007. *Standards for the 21st-
Century Learner*. http://www.ala.org/ala/mgrps/divs/aasl/guideline
sandstandards/learningstandards/AASL_LearningStandards.pdf.

Association of College and Research Libraries. 2000. *Information Literacy
Competency Standards for Higher Education*. January 18. http://www.
ala.org/ala/mgrps/divs/acrl/standards/standards.pdf.

Dawkins, Richard. 1986. *The Blind Watchmaker*. 1st ed. New York: Norton.

de Kunder, Maurice. 2011. "Google: Last Month." *The Size of the World Wide
Web*. March 30. http://www.worldwidewebsize.com.

Dempsey, Judy. 2011. "German Defense Minister Karl-Theodor zu
Guttenberg Resigns." *The New York Times* (March 1). http://
www.nytimes.com/2011/03/02/world/europe/02germany.
html?scp=1&sq=Karl-Theodor%20zu%20Guttenberg&st=cse.

Familial Hypercholesterolemia. 2011. *Wikipedia, The Free
Encyclopedia*. December 13, 2011. http://en.wikipedia.org/wiki/
Familial_hypercholesterolemia#Screening.

Fishman, Stephen. 2008. *The Public Domain: How to Find and Use Copyright-
Free Writings, Music, Art & More*. 4th ed. Berkeley: Nolo.

Foundation for Critical Thinking. 1997. *Critical Thinking: Basic Theory and
Instructional Structures*. Wye Mills, MD: Foundation for Critical
Thinking.

Gillispie, Charles, ed. 1970. Boole, George. In *Dictionary of Scientific Biography*. New York: Scribner.

Gleick, James. 2011. *The Information: A History, a Theory, a Flood*. 1st ed.
New York: Pantheon Books.

Gross, Melissa, and Don Latham. 2007. "Attaining Information Literacy: An Investigation of the Relationship Between Skill Level, Self-Estimates of Skill, and Library Anxiety." *Library & Information Science Research (07408188)* 29 (3): 332–353. doi:10.1016/j.lisr.2007.04.012. http://search.ebscohost.com.proxy.li.suu.edu:2048/login.aspx?direct=true&db=lxh&AN=26680519&site=ehost-live.

Humanities. 2011. *Merriam-Webster Dictionary*. http://www.merriam-webster.com/dictionary/humanities.

Information. 2003. *McGraw-Hill Dictionary of Scientific and Technical Terms*. 6th ed. New York: McGraw-Hill.

Intellectual Property. 2011. *Wikipedia, The Free Encyclopedia*. December 13, 2011. http://en.wikipedia.org/wiki/Intellectual_property.

Janssen, Sarah, ed. 2010. "Mars." In *The World Almanac and Book of Facts, 2011*, 347. New York: World Almanac Books.

Library of Congress Classification. 2011. *Wikipedia, The Free Encyclopedia*. December 13, 2011. http://en.wikipedia.org/wiki/Library_of_Congress_Classification.

Literate. 2011. *Dictionary.com*. http://dictionary.reference.com/browse/literate.

Mars. 2010. *The New Encyclopædia Britannica*. Chicago: Encyclopædia Britannica.

McBrien, J. Lynn, and Ronald S. Brandt. 1997. *The Language of Learning: A Guide to Education Terms*. Alexandria, VA: Association for Supervision and Curriculum Development.

Moroz, Vassili. 2001. "Mars: Atmosphere." In *Encyclopedia of Astronomy and Astrophysics*, ed. Paul Murdin. New York: Institute of Physics Publishing.

Per Capita Consumption of Major Food Commodities: 1980–2008. 2011. *The 2011 Statistical Abstract*. January 6. http://www.census.gov/compendia/statab/.

Petress, Ken. 2004. "Critical Thinking: An Extended Definition." *Education (Chula Vista, Calif.)* 124 (3): 461–66. http://vnweb.hwwilsonweb.com.proxy.li.suu.edu:2048/hww/results/getResults.jhtml?_DARGS=/hww/results/results_common.jhtml.37.

Primary. 2011. *Merriam-Webster Online Dictionary*. http://www.merriam-webster.com/dictionary/primary?show=0&t=1298045655.

Richter Magnitude Scale. 2011. *Wikipedia, The Free Encyclopedia*. February 11, 2011. http://en.wikipedia.org/wiki/Richter_scale.

Riddell, Thelma. 2007. "Critical Assumptions: Thinking Critically About Critical Thinking." *Journal of Nursing Education* 46 (3): 121–26. http://vnweb.hwwilsonweb.com.proxy.li.suu.edu:2048/hww/results/getResults.jhtml?_DARGS=/hww/results/results_common.jhtml.37.

Ruxton, Carrie. 2010. "Recommendations for the Use of Eggs in the Diet." *Nursing Standard* 24 (37): 47–55.

Text of Creative Commons Attribution-ShareAlike 3.0 Unported License. 2011. *Wikipedia, The Free Encyclopedia.* May 27. http://en.wikipedia.org/ wiki/Wikipedia:Text_of_Creative_Commons_Attribution-Share Alike_3.0_Unported_License.

U. S. Copyright Office. 2008. "Copyright Basics." *United States Copyright Office,* July. http://www.copyright.gov/circs/circ1.pdf.

U. S. Copyright Office. 2009. "Fair Use." *U.S. Copyright Office–Fair Use.* November. http://www.copyright.gov/fls/fl102.html.

UNESCO. 2003. *The Prague Declaration: Towards an Information Literate Society.* http://portal.unesco.org/ci/en/ev.php-URL_ID=19636&URL_ DO=DO_TOPIC&URL_SECTION=201.html.

World Intellectual Property Organizatioin. 2011. "What is Intellectual Property?" *World Intellectual Property Organizatioin.* June 28. http://www. wipo.int/about-ip/en/.

Index

abstract, 17
abstract databases, 46
Academic Search Premier, 23
accrediting agency, 3
accuracy, 70
advanced search, 24, 52
American Association of School
    Librarians, 4
American Psychological Association,
    85
And (Boolean operator), 21, 27, 28, 53
    And implied, 51
annotation, 17
anthropology, 9
APA style, 85
art, 9
Association of College and Research
    Libraries, 2
asterisk, 33
astronomy, 9
authority, 72
authors, 72, 73
author searching, 40
autobiography, 11

background sources, 8, 14
basic search, 24, 51

bibliographies, 17
bibliography, 85
billboards, 1
Bing, 17, 22, 51
biography, 11
biology, 9
blind submissions, 72
books, 9, 14
Boolean operators, 21, 27
Boole, George, 27
borrowing library, 59
broaden, 28, 32, 35
browse, 41
browse search, 40
business, 9

call number, 40
*Cambridge Illustrated Dictionary of
    Astronomy*, 14
chemistry, 9
Chicago Tribune, 17
circulating collection, 40
citation, 17, 85
citation databases, 46
citation information, 43
citation managers, 48, 54, 87
citation style, 85

citing sources, 84, 85
commercial databases, 23
communicating Information, 81
conclusion, 78
conference, 9
consortium, 58
contact information, 73
controlled vocabulary, 26
copyright, 82, 83
Creative Commons License, 83
credentials, 73
critical thinkers, 61
critical thinking, 61, 62
current information, 12
Cutter numbers, 42

dance, 9
data, 1
database, 21
databases, 17
   databases full text, 17
database searching, 23
database selection, 63
decimal numbers, 41, 42
depth, 13, 68
Dewey Decimal Classification, 41
diaries, 11
dictionary, 13
Directory of Open Access
   Journals, 23
distribution, 13
Dogpile, 53
domains, 53
double quotation marks, 31

EasyBib, 43, 86
eBooks, 39, 43
EBSCOhost, 23
editorialize, 69
editorials, 16
editors, 72
Edmunds, 2
electronic format, 12

Encyclopedia of Astronomy and
   Astrophysics, 71
EndNote, 43, 87
entertain, 69
eReference, 39
eReference books, 43
ethical use of information, 82
evaluation, 61
Evernote, 43

Facebook, 1
fact checking, 71, 72
fair use, 83
federated searching, 46, 53
fee databases, 23
field, 21
field searching, 40, 53
four factors, 83
free databases, 22
full bibliographic information,
   85
full text databases, 46

Google, 17, 22, 51
government documents, 83
grammar, 78
grammar checkers, 78

Harvard Business Review, 72
help screens, 34
historical information, 12
holds, 40
humanities, 9
hybrid databases, 46
hypothesis, 7

ILL. *See* interlibrary loan
indexes, 9, 17
inform, 69
information, 1, 67
   information access, 9
   information categories, 10
   information creation, 2, 9

information evaluation, 61
information formats, 12
information sources, 1
information literacy, 2
information literacy importance
of, 3
information literacy outcomes, 5
Information Literacy Competency
Standards for Higher
Education, 2
information literacy instruction, 58
information need, 2, 7
information process, 9
information sources
information sources types, 13
Institute of Museum and Library
Services, 4
intellectual property, 82
interlibrary loan, 58
Internet, 1, 13
Internet search engines, 51
in-text citation, 85
invisible web, 23

journals, 9, 16
journals open access, 23

keywords, 25, 63
keyword searching, 25
knowledge
knowledge three categories, 9

language, 9
lending library, 59
letters, 11
librarians, 57
library anxiety, 57
library catalog, 39
library instruction, 58
Library of Congress Classification, 41
limiters, 52
limiting, 52
link resolver, 46

literate, 2
literature, 9, 12
logic, 78

magazines, 16
Marie Claire, 16
*McGraw-Hill Encyclopedia of
Science and Technology*, 14
metasearch engines, 53
Microsoft Word, 43, 87
Middle States Association of
Colleges and Schools, 3
MLA Handbook, 85
MLA style, 85
Modern Language Association, 85

narrow, 28, 30, 35
National Commission on Libraries
and Information Science. *See*
Institute of Museum and Library
Services
National Forum on Information
Literacy, 4
nesting, 30, 31
New Encyclopædia Britannica, 14, 71
New England Association of Schools
and Colleges, 3
news sources, 15
NLM Gateway, 21
Not (Boolean operator), 21, 27, 30, 53
notes, 85
note taking, 43

OneNote, 43
OpenOffice.org Writer, 43, 87
Or (Boolean operator), 21, 27, 28, 29,
32, 53
order of execution, 31, 32
organization, 77
outline, 77
*Oxford Handbook of Philosophy of
Emotion*, 14
Oxford University Press, 72

paintings, 9
paraphrasing, 84, 85
parentheses, 32
peer review, 11, 72
persuade, 69
philosophy, 9
phrase searching, 31, 52, 53
physical format, 12
physics, 9
plagiarism, 84
plagiarism detection, 84
Pocket Style Manual, 86
popular information, 11
Prague Declaration, The, 4
primary information, 10, 11
print, 13
print holdings, 47
printing, 13
product, 61, 77
proofreading, 78
ProQuest Newspapers, 17
proximity operators, 30
proximity searching, 30
psychology, 9, 12
Publication Manual, 86
public domain, 83
publishers, 72
purpose, 67

quoting, 43, 84

record, 21
records, marking, 47
reference collection, 40
reference desk, 57
reference sources, 14
refine a search, 34
RefWorks, 87
relevance, 23, 32, 67
relevancy ranking, 52
Research and Documentation Online, 86
research paper, 61, 77
research process, 61, 62

research question, 7, 64
    research question refining, 8
results list, 23
retrieval, 23, 32
reviews, 16
Richter scale, 7
Rolling Stone, 16, 23
Routledge Encyclopedia of Philosophy, 14

scholarly articles, 16
scholarly information, 11
science, 9
scope, 13, 68
search results, 23
search statement, 27, 62
search terms, 24
secondary information, 10
self-citations, 71
social science, 9
sociology, 9, 12
Son of Citation Machine, 86
spell checkers, 78
spelling, 78
Standards for the 21st-Century Learner, 4
stop words, 21
style, 68
subject searching, 26, 40
subject-specific database, 45
subject terms, 40
summarizing, 84, 85
synonyms, 25, 29

television, 1
terms of use, 83
theater, 9
thesis, 7
timeliness, 70
Time magazine, 11, 16
title searching, 40
truncation, 32, 52
Turnitin, 84
Twitter, 1

UNESCO, 4
using information, 82

validity, 70
Venn diagrams, 28
visible web, 22

Wikipedia, 14
wildcards, 33

word processors, 78, 86
*World Almanac and Book of Facts,
2011,* 71

year of publication, 42
YouTube, 9

Zotero, 43, 87

About the Author

Scott Lanning received his Master's of Library Science from Northern Illinois University. He has been a reference librarian throughout his long career, providing library instruction to students as part of his jobs. He currently teaches reference services and information literacy courses at Southern Utah University. Scott is also the co-author of *Essential Reference Services for Today's School Media Specialists,* which is now in its second edition.